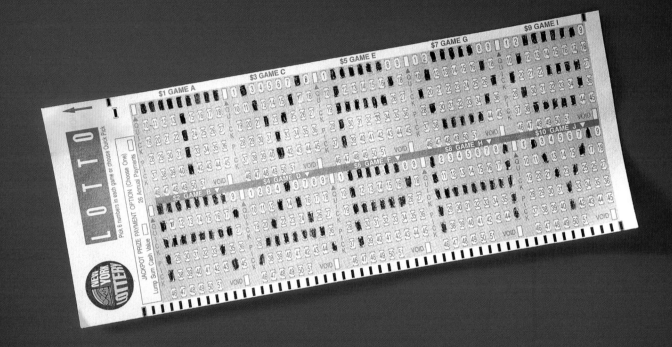

2 2

The
Annual
of the
TYPE
DIRECTORS
CLUB

THE ANNUAL OF THE TYPE DIRECTORS CLUB

forty-seventh exhibition

FIRST PUBLISHED IN 2001 IN
THE UNITED STATES BY HBI,
AN IMPRINT OF HARPERCOLLINS
PUBLISHERS.
10 EAST 53RD STREET
NEW YORK, NY 10022-5299

DISTRIBUTED IN THE U.S. AND CANADA BY
WATSON-GUPTILL PUBLICATIONS
770 BROADWAY
NEW YORK, NY 10003-9595
TEL: (800) 451-1741
OR (732) 363-4511 IN NJ, AK, HI
FAX: (732) 363-0338
ISBN 0-8230-5557-4

DISTRIBUTED THROUGHOUT THE
REST OF THE WORLD BY
HARPERCOLLINS INTERNATIONAL
10 EAST 53RD STREET
NEW YORK, NY 10022-5299
FAX: 212 207-7654
ISBN 0-06-018586-4

THE LIBRARY OF CONGRESS
HAS CATALOGED THIS SERIAL TITLE
AS FOLLOWS:
TYPOGRAPHY (TYPE DIRECTORS CLUB (U.S.))
TYPOGRAPHY: THE ANNUAL OF THE
TYPE DIRECTORS CLUB. -/-
NEW YORK: HBI
2001-ANNUAL.

TYPOGRAPHY (NEW YORK, NY)
1. PRINTING, PRACTICAL - PERIODICALS.
2. GRAPHIC ARTS - PERIODICALS.
1. TYPE DIRECTORS CLUB (U.S.)

MANUFACTURED IN HONG KONG.

ACKNOWLEDGMENTS

The Type Directors Club gratefully
acknowledges the following for
their support and contributions to
the success of TDC 47 and TDC² 2001:

DESIGN: GAIL ANDERSON
         KEN DELAGO
STILL LIFE PHOTOGRAPHY: BOB GRANT
         (WWW.GRANTPIX.COM)
EDITING: SUSAN E. DAVIS

JUDGING FACILITIES: SCHOOL OF
VISUAL ARTS
EXHIBITION FACILITIES: THE 2 WEST
13 STREET GALLERY, PARSONS
SCHOOL OF DESIGN
CHAIRPERSONS' AND JUDGES' PHOTOS:
FRAN COLLINS
HISTORY SECTION TYPE COURTESY OF
AMY UNIKEWICZ, JELLY ASSOCIATES
(WWW.JELLYASSOCIATES.COM)
TDC MEDAL: GERARD HUERTA

TDC 47 COMPETITION (CALL FOR ENTRIES):
DESIGN: GAIL ANDERSON
PRINTER: ANDERSON LITHOGRAPH,
LOS ANGELES, CALIFORNIA
PAPER: NEENAH PAPER
PREPRESS: A TO A GRAPHIC SERVICES, INC.

TDC² 2001 COMPETITION (CALL FOR ENTRIES)
DESIGN: JOHN D. BERRY
PRINTER: QUALITY HOUSE OF GRAPHICS
PREPRESS: HORAN IMAGING SOLUTIONS
PAPER: MEAD COATED PAPERS

The principal typeface used
in the composition of TYPOGRAPHY 22
is **EPLICA**

CONTENTS

YPE DIRECTORS CLUB

BY KLAUS SCHMIDT

DURING THE 1940s letterpress was the norm for quality printing, while rotogravure was used predominately for mass circulation periodicals. If one could not afford the best, there was always offset lithography — a bit flat and gray but great on uncoated paper and tight budgets. Art directors worked with new typefaces, such as Bernhard Modern, Fairfield, and Lydian. For commercial design and advertising, type was set by hand or on quality machinery like Monotype but less frequently on linecasters in specialized typesetting plants. In the 40s more than 50 advertising typography shops in America belonged to the Advertising Typographers Association. Many of them were centered on East 45th Street in New York, which was nicknamed Ad Type Alley. ᘘᘘᘘᘘᘘᘘᘘ

In the spring of 1943 Pete Tolles of J. Walter Thompson Advertising Agency and his assistant, Frank Powers, invited a few colleagues as well as Ed Rondthaler and Harold Horman, pioneers of Photolettering Inc., to an informal luncheon to talk about their favorite subject: type. This informal group grew, meeting a few more times before the end of the year. Upon Pete's untimely death in 1944, Frank Powers took over. He envisioned a more dynamic role for the group, and the casual gatherings led to the formation of the Type Directors Club (TDC) in October 1946 with Frank as president. Frank and his good friend, Jim Secrest, coined the new term "type director" to identify their special relationship with the typographic arts. Before that typographers who worked in ad agencies were either specialized production people or art directors, sometimes called "typographic art directors."

Charter members of the TDC were Arnold Bank, Alfred Dickman, Glenn Foss, John Lord, Frank Merriman, Gerard O'Neill, Frank Power, Ed Rondthaler, James Secrest, William Seculer, Joseph Weiler, Hal Zamboni, and Milton Zudeck, soon followed by Freeman (Jerry) Craw, Ed Gottschall, and others.

In 1947 the first of many programs,

the art
and
science
of
typography

world seminar and exhibition · april 26, 1958 · type directors club

held at the AD Gallery of the Composing Room, was sponsored by the young club. There were ten "Type Talks" by prominent club members, ranging in subject matter from "Type Recognition" to "Individualism in Typography." This lecture series was followed a year later by a second one at the Wilkie Memorial Building. By 1949 the ten talks were an institution, and the TDC continued its lecture series in one form or another under different headings throughout the 50s.

During the beginning of that decade, Caledonia and Times New Roman had joined the typographic hit parade. Film typesetting on devices like the Intertype Fotosetter, the Monophoto, and the Lumitype or Photon introduced the world of possibilities in photographic composition (which had actually been experimented with since the 1890s).

In the early 50s the TDC held it first show, limited to members. Later in the decade, the annual competition was opened to nonmembers and finally to participants from all over the world. The first printed catalog (of the second competition) was issued in 1956. Besides being distributed by the club, the TDC's modestly printed, black-and-white catalogs were carried in *Art Direction* magazine.

In April 1956 a TDC forum entitled "Inspired Typography 1966," took up the question of design, typography, and visual communication in relation to socioeconomic and scientific developments of the future. There were statements by designers from fourteen countries besides the United States. Some of the papers, as well as later presentations at TDC seminars, resulted in the book, *Typographic Directions*, edited by Ed Gottchall, designed by Herb Lubalin, and published by *Art Direction*.

1957 saw the end of the initial lecture programs. The windup, held at the Hotel Shelton in New York, was presided over by Alfred Dickman under the the title "What's New?" Then in 1958 the TDC expanded its program format, holding the first World Seminar, "The Art and Science of Typography." On April 26, more than 500 designers and type-minded people congregated at the Silvermine Artist Guild in Connecticut for the seminar, chaired by the eminent Will Burtin. The panel consisted of Ottl Aicher from Germany, Max Huber from Italy, Yusaku Kamekura from Japan, Willem Sandberg from Holland, Herbert Spencer from England, and Bruce McKenzie and Anatol Rappaport from the United States. The all-day event was accompanied by two exhibitions: almost 200 designs that had been awarded Certificates of Typographic Excellence in the club's fourth annual competition and a collection of outstanding work by designers all over the international scene. Several days later additional parts of the program were held at the World Affairs Center in New York, with panel discussions by professionals like Lester Beall, Freeman Craw, Hunter Middleton, and Cipe Pineless.

To wind up the 50s the TDC conducted the "Typography USA" forum with the subtitle, "What's New in American Typography." Held at the New York Biltmore Hotel, the all-star, one-day event was planned by the Club's educational chairman Aaron Burns and moderated by Will Burtin. The distinguished panel included Saul Bass, Herbert Bayer, Lou Dorfsman, Alvin Eisenman, Gene Federico, William Golden, Morton Goldscholl, Allen Hurlburt, Leo Lionni, Herb Lubalin, Paul Rand, Ladislav Sutnar, and Brad Thompson.

In the 1950s the TDC was still a small local or, at best, regional organization. In 1956 the first printed catalog of its annual show listed 71 members. But it was beginning to make a worldwide impression. The famous German type designer Hermann Zapf had been named an honorary member in 1952. He was followed by members John Dreyfus in England, Austin Grandjean in Denmark, G. W. Ovink in Holland, and in the mid-sixties Olaf Leu and Kurt Weidemann in Germany. By the time the club's first annual book, *Typography 1*, was published in 1980, the TDC's membership had risen to 174. Today there are 650 members, of whom 200 reside outside the New York metropolitan area and 230 in foreign countries. Thus the TDC became a truly international society.

The 50s and 60s were turbulent times for typography. Helvetica and the Swiss School vied for popularity with revivals in Art Noveau, Art Deco, and America's Western style. Psychedelic type became a new wave, and metal type was losing the battle to photocomposition. The Alphatype became the initial choice among typesetting companies in American design and

advertising centers, later followed by the phototypesetting equipment of Compugraphic, Intertype, Linotype, Monotype, and other manufacturers. Two-inch film fonts were used to set most of the display copy, while Photolettering, with its Rutherford machines, as well as "process lettering" houses held their ground.

Through the 1960s the TDC continued to grow in stature. An evening lecture series was held at the World Affairs Center in 1960 under program chairman Edward Gottschall. A study of typographic trends, published in 1961, was based on a four-page questionnaire with 44 questions, sent to 3,200 typographers and art directors in North America. "Type Whys" was the title of a 1962 seminar. "Source 63," chaired by Ed Gottschall, saw about 300 participants jammed into the Hotel Shelton, viewing film trailers, slides, and outstanding TV commercials. No talks, no panels, just a day of inspiring graphics.

Besides its conspicuous lecture series, seminars, and annual award competitions and shows, the TDC conducted weekly – later biweekly and still later monthly – Tuesday luncheons,

ABOVE: ANNOUNCEMENT FOR 1956 TDC FORUM "INSPIRED TYPOGRAPHY 1966." DESIGNER AARON BURNS. LOWER LEFT: ANNOUNCEMENT FOR LUNCHEON PRESENTATION BY STEVEN HELLER ON LUCIAN BERNHARD. DESIGNER LOUISE FILI.

hosting speakers and guests from the United States as well as from across the Atlantic. These luncheons, held at the Roger Smith Hotel on Lexington Avenue, at the SUNY Graduate Center on Bryant Park, and finally at the Art Directors Club, presented lectures, films, slides, and demos. And they were full of good professional camaraderie.

In 1966 under President Eugene Ettenberg's leadership and arranged by Horace Hart, a group of TDC members toured Europe, with stops in London and Paris and side tours to Copenhagen, Madrid, Siena, and Zurich. Most memorable was

The 22nd Annual New York Type Directors Club Exhibit Catalog.

the dinner at the Wynkyn de Worde Society in London.

By the mid-60s TDC activities were extended to Europe. In 1965 the club's annual show, TDC11, was exhibited for the first time in central Europe, arranged by TDC member Olaf Leu of Frankfurt, Germany, who became the club's first international liaison. He was later joined by additional contact members from England, France, Japan, Mexico, South America, Sweden, Switzerland, and Vietnam. Today the TDC show is featured in numerous design centers at schools, graphic arts companies, trade fairs (like DRUPA), and graphic arts conventions in many parts of the world: throughout North and South America, Europe, Australia, New Zealand, and Eastern Asia. It has become one of the most respected and eagerly awaited mirrors on typographic trends on the globe.

Up until 1971 the annual TDC show in New York was exhibited in various locations. That year the show moved to the AIGA Gallery and, ten years later, to the ITC where it remained through the 80s. After that it moved to the gallery of The

Cooper Union and, lately, to Parsons School of Design.

Hermann Zapf became the first recipient of the TDC Medal in 1967. In succeeding years this honor was bestowed on type designers R. Hunter Middleton, Georg Trump, Adrian Frutiger, Freeman Craw, Ed Benguiat, Matthew Carter, Colin Brignall, and Günter Gerhard Lange. The TDC Medal was also awarded to

calligraphers Arnold Bank and Paul Standard, to eminent graphic designers like Herb Lubalin, Paul Rand, Lou Dorfsman, Bradbury Thompson, and Gene Federico, to *Rolling Stone* magazine, and to those who had greatly fostered the club and the typographic arts like TDC's founder Frank Powers, Dr. Robert Leslie, Edward Rondthaler, and Aaron Burns.

During the decades of the 60s and 70s the results of the annual TDC Typographic Excellence competitions, always judged by panels of distinguished designers and typographic practitioners, began to be published as increasingly more elegant catalogs. Early in the 70s, the TDC also published a keepsake marking its 25th anniversary. It contained a thumbnail history of the club that concluded with the words, "One wonders what the club's 50th history anniversary will read like. What names will be in it? What will the world of typography and printing be like then?" As a matter of fact, the 50th anniversary of the TDC in 1996 was celebrated in New York City with many new and old members, a good number of past presidents, and even some of the founders in the audience.

In 1980 the winners of the TDC's annual Typographic Excellence Competition (then in its 26th year) were for the first

time published in book form with full-color illustrations as *Typography 1*, the Annual of the Type Directors Club by Watson-Guptill Publications. Since that year, the TDC's annuals, published lately by Hearst International Books, have become standard reference works for measuring typographic design trends on a worldwide scale. They are collected in private and institutional libraries in many countries.

In late 1982 Jerry Singleton, TDC's executive secretary for over 20 years, retired, and Bernhard Ellis of Jules Schwimmer Associates took over for a year. Then Carol Wahler, who became the club's secretary in the summer of 1983, was promoted to executive director, administering TDC's business affairs to this day.

In the technology arena 1983 saw the introduction of Adobe PostScript. Two years later Apple introduced the Macintosh and the LaserWriter printer, Aldus released PageMaker 1.0, and Paul Brainard coined the term "desk top publishing" (DTP). DTP became the most incisive development in the prepress field, "democratizing" typographic production by putting it squarely in the hands of the designer and art director and, for the most part, taking it out of the realm of specialized graphic arts shops. During the decade of the 80s the TDC was one of the first organizations to run seminars on desk top publishing. Speakers at these events included Paul Brainard, Frank Romano, and John Warnock. Also in 1983 the TDC published its first newsletter, "Gutenberg & Sons," which later became "Gutenberg & Family" and finally today's "LetterSpace."

The Type Directors Club hosted "Type '87," which coincided with the ATypI (Association Graphique Internationale) Congress of that year in New York City. Heralded as "a world's fair of type," it featured speakers such as Ed Benguiat, Chuck Bigelow, Adrian Frutiger, Günter Gerhard Lange, and Hermann Zapf, as well as Neville Brody's first appearance in the United States.

At the beginning of the 21st century, the Type Directors Club, having served the art, science, and technology of typography for over 50 years, is not just an organization for type directors, nor is it limited to the New York area. The club represents just about every aspect of type and typographic communication and is truly an international organization; its membership includes professionals and students from over 31 countries. The club is now engaged in cultural exchanges with organizations like the Typographic Circle in London, hosting multimedia conferences, and sponsoring news items about the typographic world on the Internet.

Some things, however, have not changed: the club's commitment to the typographic arts, its dedication to education, and its continued striving to promote typographic excellence in all forms of graphic communication in printed as well as electronic media.

Founded when type was a piece of metal that could be picked up, held in the palm of one's hand, and admired as a piece of sculpture, the Type Directors Club has remained true to the heritage of typographic communication while embracing cutting-edge technology and graphic expression. The club has expanded its small fraternal beginnings into a world-class organization for everyone who works with, studies, and creates — or just loves — type.

ABOVE: "ANNOUNCE-MENT FOR METAMOR-PHOSIS," A TDC CONFER-ENCE ON MAY 18, 1998. DESIGNER DAVE T. HO. BELOW: TDC NEWS-LETTER, LETTERSPACE. DESIGNER JAMES MONTALBANO.

TDC MEDALIST

*The Type Directors Club Medal
is awarded to individuals and institutions
that have made significant advances for,
contributions to, and achievements in
the art and craft of type and typography.*

OLIN BRIGNALL

A TYPE DESIGNER, art director, and photographer born in 1940 in Warwickshire, England, Colin Brignall started his career as a commercial photo~ grapher for the fashion trade, the press, and industry. In the early 60s he joined the Letraset Type Studio as a photographic technician, and in 1974 he advanced to type designer for Letraset International. Since 1980 Brignall has been type director of Esselte Letraset in London. ∾ ∾ ∾

Two of his early typeface designs are still among the most enduring display faces in use today: Aachen Bold and Revue. The former, for instance, can be seen all over the French port of Calais on its city and harbor signage, while Revue is extensively employed in sports labeling and identity.

Colin Brignall is the creator of more than 100 alphabets. During the 70s and 80s he designed typefaces for text as well as display, including Corinthian, Edwardian, Italia, Octopuss, Premier Lightline, Premier Shaded, Romic, and Superstar. His letterforms have survived the technological transition from phototypography and transfer lettering to today's digital composition.

Throughout his career Brignall has encouraged and inspired young designers to create typefaces for the Letraset dry transfer process and as digital fonts. Under Brignall's direction and supervision, the Letraset studio produced more than 500 original typefaces between 1970 and 1996. An equal number of fonts were developed and issued by the International Typeface Corporation (ITC) of New York between 1985 and 2000 when Brignall was a member of the ITC review board and, since 1996, ITC's director of type development.

Colin Brignall has worked with several generations of type icons – from David Kindersley and Hermann Zapf to Ed Benguiat, Matthew Carter, Phill Grimshaw, and Summer Stone. He has written and lectured extensively about type design as well as typographic and graphic design at academic institutions and before typographic societies. After Brignall's recent lecture at England's Yorkshire South Coast College of Art and Design, the school decided to establish an annual Colin Brignall Student Award, reflecting both his prestige and his contribution to contemporary type design, which has influenced whole generations of designers.   ∾

Figural Book
ABCDEFGHIJKLMNOPQRSTUVWXYZ
abcdefghijklmnopqrstuvwxyz
1234567890

Aachen Bold
ABCDEFGHIJKLMNOPQRSTUVWXYZ
abcdefghijklmnopqrstuvwxyz
1234567890

ÜNTER GERHARD LANGE

TYPOGRAPHER, TEACHER, type designer, and long-time artistic director of the highly respected German type foundry, H. Berthold AG, Günter Gerhard Lange, aka GGL, was born in the eastern German city of Frankurt an der Oder. After severe injuries released him from the German army in World War II, he attended the Akademie für Graphische Künste und Buchgewerbe (Academy of the Graphic Arts and Printing Trades) in Leipzig from 1941 to 1945. He was a student of Prof. Georg Bélwe and, after graduation, assistant to well-known type designer Walter Tiemann until 1949 when he undertook advanced studies at the Hochschule für Bildende Künste (College of fine Arts) in Berlin. A year later Lange joined the Berthold type foundry, first, as a freelance consultant and, from 1961 until 1990, as its artistic director, responsible for the firm's entire type program. ∾ ∾ ∾ ∾

Lange's teaching career began in 1955 at the Meisterschule für Grafik und Buchgewerbe (Master School for Graphics and the Printing Trades) in Berlin where he taught for five years. He has been an instructor and lecturer at graphic arts schools in Hamburg, Leipzig, Munich, and Vienna. Lange is an honorary member of the German Art Directors Club. In 1989 he received the Frederick W. Goudy Award from the Rochester Institute of Technology.

Lange's extensive lecturing in Germany and abroad has brought him wide recognition as a teacher of young graphic and typographic designers and practitioners. Articles written by him have appeared in numerous technical and design periodicals and books. Frequently books designed by him have been selected as some of the "Most Beautiful Books" in Germany.

As H. Berthold AG's artistic director and member of its management team, Günter Gerhard Lange was responsible for the creation and the meticulous production and quality standards reflected in each of the fine Berthold typefaces. He presided over a huge program of typographic revivals and adaptations and was personally responsible for versions of well-known classic letterforms like Baskerville, Bodoni, Caslon, Deepdene, Garamond, and others during the transition periods from metal to photographic and computerized typesetting.

Lange also designed such original fonts, such as Arena, Bodoni Old Face, Boulevard, Champion, Concord, Derby, El Greco, Franklin Antique, Imago, and Nova, to name a few. Lange's unique skills, his vast expertise, and his never-ceasing attention to craftsmanship elevated Berthold's type program to one of the most significant and highly revered type libraries in the typographic world. That was in addition to Berthold's precision typesetting equipment like the widely used Diatype and Diatronic.

In 1990, however, H. Berthold AG foundered on the rocks of the digital revolution, despite manufacturing photographic and computerized typesetting machinery for many decades. Currently digital versions of its fonts are marketed by Berthold Types Ltd. of Chicago, and Günter Gerhard Lange, now over 80 years "young," is acting as a consultant to that new company, which continues to carry the old, well-respected name of one of Germany's finest type foundries.   ∾

ARENA NEW

Günter Gerhard Lange
1951–54

abcdefghijklmnopqrstuvwxyz
ABCDEFGHIJKLMNOP
QRSTUVWXYZ1234567890
1234567890
ABCDEFGHIJKLMNOPQRSTUVWXYZ

Berthold's quick brown fox jumps ov
Berthold's quick brown fox jum
Berthold's quick brown fox jumps over
Berthold's quick brown fox jum
Berthold's quick brown fox jumps ov
Berthold's quick brown fox jumps
Berthold's quick brown fox jumps
Berthold's quick brown fox jumps
Berthold's quick brown fox jumps

WHITTINGHAM

Günter Gerhard Lange
Dieter Hofrichter
2000

abcdefghijklmnopqrstuvwxyz
ABCDEFGHIJKLMNOP
QRSTUVWXYZ€1234567890
1234567890
ABCDEFGHIJKLMNOPQRSTUVWXYZ

Berthold's quick brown fox jumps
Berthold's quick brown fox jum
Berthold's quick brown fox jumps ov
Berthold's quick brown fox jumps
Berthold's quick brown fox jumps
Berthold's quick brown fox jump
Berthold's quick brown fox jump

ITC

Paul Souza

TYPOGRAPHY 22
The Judges
TYPOGRAPHY 22

RICHARD BAKER

Matthew Carter

LYNN STALEY

WENDY RICHMOND

ROBYNNE Raye

JONATHAN HOEFLER

SOMEWHERE between the new economy, the new mil~ lennium, and the new new thing, type is experiencing a renaissance. More than ever, we rely on its ability to express and contain ideas and messages.

Communication is fast. Whether we're sending or receiving. There's a demand for stripped-down clarity, an economy of means.

In recent years, designers have achieved high status on communication's cutting edge. How have we been respond~ ing to the need for speed? Do we employ type as our greatest ally — whether it is printed or transmitted, wired or wireless — for communicating in the clearest, most efficient manner?

In this new age, does excellence in typography re~ ally matter, or is it a quaint notion from the past?

Is our goal to slow readers down or speed them up?

What difference does the shape of a letter make?

How does the position and placement of words on a sur~ face alter our perception?

What do we hope to accomplish by focusing on this aspect of design?

The answers lie in looking hard at excellent work.

E-NETWORKING SOLUTIONS FOR BUSINESS

VOLUME 2, NUMBER 1 SPRING 2001

Robert
Reich on
the new
economy

Stan Davis
on the next
economy

full speed
ahead

PLUS
CRM: A winning
recipe for the
restaurant trade
MANAGING MONEY:
The Web brings
401(k) plans to small
businesses
E-GOVERNMENT:
A registry of motor
vehicles accelerates
just about everything

GENUiTY™

RONN CAMPISI specializes in publication design. He is the former design director of *The Boston Globe* and has also served as design director of *Boston* magazine, *The Real Paper,* and *Fusion* magazine.

He has won more than 300 awards for his work. In 1983 he was the designer and part of the team that won a Pulitzer Prize for a special magazine section entitled "War and Peace in the Nuclear Age."

His Boston-based studio, Ronn Campisi Design, has designed the formats for many of the leading technology magazines and newspapers published in America, including *Computer Reseller News, Computerworld, InfoWorld,* and *PC Magazine.*

He currently art directs and designs magazines for Boston Ballet, EMC Corporation, The Federal Reserve Bank of Boston, Genuity, Progress Software, and Smith College.

Jamaican-born R I C H A R D B A K E R, a graduate of Manhattan's School of Vi-sual Arts, has worked at *US*, *Vibe*, *The Washington Post Sunday Magazine* and is currently art director at *Premiere*. Heralded as one of the most influential people in publishing by *Folio* magazine, he has received awards from the Society of Publication Designers.

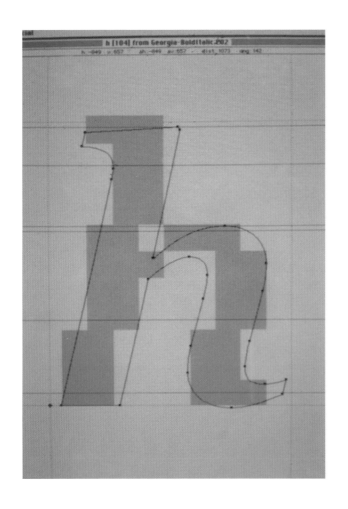

MATTHEW CARTER is a type designer with forty years experience with typographic technologies, ranging from hand-cut punches to computer fonts. He designed the typefaces Bell Centennial (for the U.S. telephone
directories), Big Caslon, ITC Galliard, Mantinia, Miller, Miller
News (for newspaper text), Shelley Script, Snell Round-
hand, Sophia, and types commissioned by Apple, Microsoft
(the screen fonts Georgia and Verdana), *Newsweek, The
Philadelphia Inquirer, Sports Illustrated, Time, U.S. News &
World Report*, the Walker Art Center, *The Washington Post*, and
Wired. He is a principal of Carter & Cone Type Inc. in Cambridge, Massachusetts,
designers and makers of original typefaces.

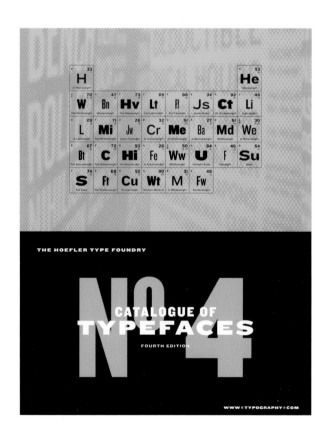

JONATHAN HOEFLER is a typeface designer and an armchair type historian whose New York studio, The Hoefler Type Foundry, specializes in the design of original typefaces. Named one of the forty most influential designers in America by *I.D. Magazine*, Hoefler's publishing work includes award-winning original typeface designs for *Esquire, Harper's Bazaar, The New York Times Magazine, Rolling Stone,* and *Sports Illustrated*; his institutional clients range from the Solomon R. Guggenheim Museum to the rock band They Might Be Giants. Perhaps his best known work is the Hoefler Text family of typefaces designed for Apple Computer and now appearing everywhere as part of the Macintosh operating system. Hoefler's work has been exhibited internationally and is included in the permanent collection of the Cooper-Hewitt National Design Museum (Smithsonian Institution) in New York.

After studying graphic design and printmaking at Western Washington University, ROBYNNE RAYE co-founded the Seattle-based studio Modern Dog when she discovered no other design firm would hire her. She first won national recognition designing posters for Seattle's fringe theatres. Fourteen years later she still designs entertainment promotions — locally and nationally — and still loves poster design best.

With a style that has been described as "adventurous," Raye has developed identity systems, packaging, illustration, and Web sites for such diverse clients as K2 Snowboards, *The New York Times*, Planet 7 Technologies, Seattle Public Health Department, Simon & Schuster, the Tacoma Art Museum, Uni-Qlo (Japan), and Yale Repertory Theatre. In addition, many of her posters are in museum collections around the world.

Over the past decade, Raye has taught design workshops and lectured extensively. She currently teaches an upper-level design class at Cornish College of the Arts in Seattle.

In 1978, with a background in art and design, **WENDY RICHMOND** began mixing traditional production with new media at MIT's Visible Language Workshop. She participated in technology start-ups and co-founded the Design Lab at WGBH TV to develop design principles for interactive media. Richmond's current work combines photography and sculpture. Her writing and teaching focus on creativity through visual media.

Richmond is the recipient of a Rockefeller Foundation residency in Bellagio, Italy, a National Endowment for the Arts grant, and numerous design and art awards. She has served on the AIGA National Board of Directors and is the author of *Design & Technology: Erasing the Boundaries*. Her column has appeared in *Communication Arts* magazine since 1983. Richmond teaches at the Harvard Graduate School of Education.

PAUL SOUZA is currently design director at Photo
Access in Seattle, a leading provider of digital imaging and
print solutions for the Internet.

Paul began his career in traditional advertising/design studio
settings, moving into television at KERA in Dallas, and later at WGBH
in Boston, where he spent sixteen years designing print, video, and multimedia.
Since 1986 Paul has focused on computer-based multimedia projects. In 1990,
Paul and colleague Wendy Richmond formed the WGBH Design Lab. Clients included Apple, Bitstream, Interleaf, Lotus, Motorola, and Prodigy. In 1993 Paul
joined Aldus Corporation as customer advocate with responsibility for identify-
ing ways to address customer needs, feature definition, and user interface design.

In 1995 Paul co-founded zero.one, an interactive marketing, design, and
technology firm. Clients included Adobe, Apple, Hewlett Packard, Safeco Insurance, and Sony Pictures Entertainment.

Paul has been a member of the board of the American Center for Design, the
Boston chapter of the American Institute of Graphic Arts, and the Aldus Graphic
Arts Advisory Board.

LYNN STALEY joined *Newsweek* as director of design in May 1995 and was named assistant managing editor in December 1995. She is responsible for the overall look of the magazine, overseeing the art, graphics, cover, and photo departments for all editions, domestic and overseas.

Lynn came to the magazine from *The Boston Globe*, where after starting as an editorial director in 1980, she worked her way up, becoming deputy managing editor and supervising a staff of more than 60 in the design, editorial systems, and photo departments. In 1989 she oversaw the redesign of the entire paper, including introduction of color. Under Staley's innovative directorship, the paper garnered more than 250 awards in five years.

Staley has earned numerous honors and professional awards, including those from the New York Art Directors Club, The Society of Newspaper Design, The Society of Publication Designers, and the Type Directors Club. She has been a frequent guest lecturer and presenter at the Poytner Institute for Media Studies on a wide range of topics. Among her extra-professional and civic activities, Staley has served as president of the Society for News Design. Staley earned a bachelor of arts from Connecticut College.

RICHARD BAKER

LOU REED HAS SCARS and I touched them. On the cover the scrawled type that is embossed on Lou Reed's self-portrait has the look and feel of scars. The design of the book is an interactive experience. It was my favorite piece in the show.

Stefan Sagmeister's design pays tribute to a collection of lyrics that span 30 years. Lou Reed's writing is simple, literate, and emotionally intense. The design of the book is edgy and experimental. The typefaces are simple and few but are used in unpredictable ways. The type is terse, impatient; it gets angry, sins, and pleads for love. And it's always moving, yet the design never gets in the way of the reader. Some of the pages have been drawn on or printed in black; each chapter is different from the next — a true record of emotional conditions.

THE COLLECTED LYRICS of Lou Reed feature a self-portrait with embossed type on the cover. The lyrics are divided into chapters according to each album. Every album has its own typographic style, reflecting the overall mood and feel of the words and the music.

The steadiness and simplicity of Lou's work are reflected in the use of one single typeface throughout the book. This typeface gets drunk, does drugs, becomes incomprehensible, dresses up, is mean, visionary, gorgeous, and glowing. It's Lou's voice.

—STEFAN SAGMEISTER, *designer*

CATEGORY	Book
DESIGN	Stefan Sagmeister, Hjalti Karlsson, and Jan Wilker *New York, New York*
LETTERING	Stefan Sagmeister, Hjalti Karlsson, and Jan Wilker
ART DIRECTION	Stefan Sagmeister
CREATIVE DIRECTION	Stefan Sagmeister
STUDIO	Sagmeister Inc.
CLIENT	Hyperion and Lou Reed
PRINCIPAL TYPE	Times and handlettering
DIMENSIONS	5³/₄ x 8¹/₂ in. (14.6 x 21.6 cm)

MATTHEW CARTER

HARD AS IT IS for a Red Sox fan to say it, I have to admit that *The New York Times* rose to the occasion of the 2000 World Series—it had been 44 years since New York played New York for the baseball championship, after all. The paper managed to cheer enthusiastically but impartially by giving equal time to Yankee fans and Mets fans to insult one another. There was practical advice, too: I remember an article aimed at young kids suggesting strategies for staying up past bedtime to watch evening games on television. The typography of the Subway Series pages was both celebratory and informative. The designer made a page-heading logo out of the New York City subway signs, Helvetica reversed out of color-coded circles, and imitated the destination boards on subway cars to give a real visual excitement to the day-to-day coverage of the build-up to the series and the games themselves. The witty sign motif did double duty, instructing subway riders on which trains to take, given that Yankee fans would otherwise get lost on the way to Shea Stadium in Queens, and no Mets fan could be expected to know where The Bronx is, let alone Yankee Stadium. The typography is, of course, an in-joke to the extent that out-of-towners reading *The Times* (or *The Type Directors Club Annual*) who have never experienced the New York City subway system will not get the references, but to criticize the paper for this would only sound like envy. Congratulations, and wait until next year, as we say in Boston.

THE CHALLENGE: capture the excitement of a Subway Series while maintaining the soft–spoken dignity of *The New York Times*. The solution: transform the daily sports cover into a makeshift subway station. The section flag adapted the color and typography of New York City subway signage, maintaining the correct colors for each train line (the A and E trains are blue, and the S train is silver). As for the letters that were not accounted for by the subway system – U, W, Y, and I – we applied colors in an impartial fashion – U and W became green to represent the No. 4 and No. 5 trains that lead to Yankee Stadium, and the Y and I became light purple for the No. 7 train to Shea Stadium. Completing the subway station motif were the stylized tokens created by digital illustrator Joe Zeff. Again fairness reigned, with each team's logo represented, following an extra-inning debate about whether to replicate the older style tokens, as we did; the present style tokens; or even a MetroCard.

—WAYNE KAMIDOI, *designer*

CATEGORY	Editorial
DESIGN	Wayne Kamidoi
	New York, New York
ILLUSTRATION	Joe Zeff
CLIENT	The New York Times
PRINCIPAL TYPE	Based on Chalet,
	Akzidenz Grotesk,
	and Helvetica
DIMENSIONS	13 x 21 3/4 in.
	(33 x 55.3 cm)

JONATHAN HOEFLER

TO BE MOVED by Chris Ware's work, it is enough to enjoy it on a superficial level. His characters inhabit a typographic pageant that chronicles the complete history of the industrial Midwest, from the fertile lettering of ragtime sheet music to the cloying graphics of the modern supermarket. He narrates in show cards and cartoon titles; his characters dream in grade school handwriting and interstitials from talkies. Yet despite Ware's seductive ability to work in period styles, he never stoops to nostalgia and is never trite or blandly ironic. Instead, he borrows from a sophisticated palette of typographic styles in order to evoke an equally complex range of atmospheres. In Ware's hands, vernaculars that have no names manage nonetheless to evoke uncannily specific moods, as precise as "equivocal regret" or "the melancholy recollection of childhood's doomed escapist fantasies."

Beneath Ware's thoughtful and adroit typography is a work of literature and a story which is told not merely through words and pictures but through design. Plots are advanced in diagrammatic interludes, themes developed through iconography. (There are also elaborate frontispieces, printed instructions, editorials, advertisements, and a cut-out— Ware clearly likes graphic design.) Most remarkably, he uses familiar graphic devices in ways that not only run counter to expectations, but are often directly antithetical to tone. There are moments when Ware subtly inflates the space between form and content in order to keep the reader at a distance: inconsequential words are rendered with great flourish, deeply moving passages are told through the affectless format of a flow chart. Ware uses design where it can't *not* be used, which is ultimately what we all aspire to do. He invests every aspect of his work with great purpose, and the results are moving, admirable, and inspiring.

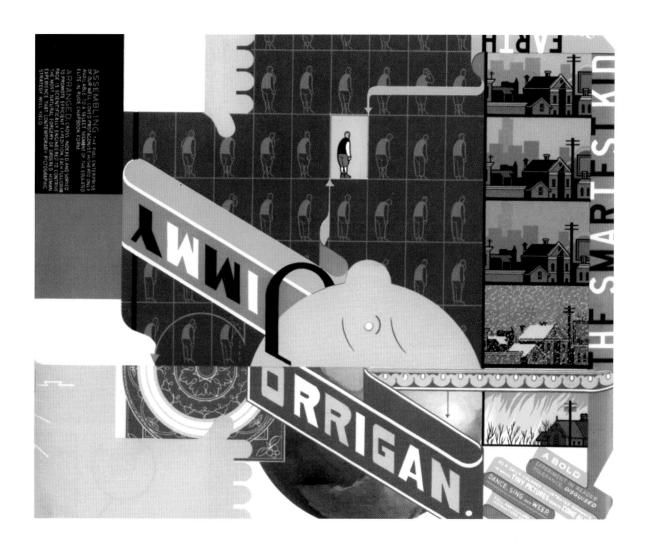

CATEGORY Book
DESIGN Chris Ware
Chicago, Illinois
LETTERING Chris Ware
ART DIRECTION Chip Kidd and Chris Ware
CLIENT Pantheon Books
PRINCIPAL TYPE Century Schoolbook
and handlettering
DIMENSIONS 8 x 7 in. (20.3 x 17.8 cm)

CHRIS WARE doesn't go for competitions, but I submitted *Jimmy Corrigan* on his behalf because I think his use of typography throughout the book is extraordinary.

Almost entirely handlettered, the work represents a level of dexterity and skill that has all but vanished in our point-and-click culture. Ware goes much further than simply mimicking the flourishes of Edwardian-era calligraphic decoration. The letterforms inhabit the design in places we aren't always used to seeing them, striking out on their own new frontier.

My deepest thanks to the judges for their consideration.

—CHIP KIDD, *designer*

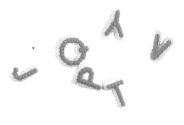

ROBYNNE RAYE

THE BULL SIGNS CALENDAR from London design studio Atélier Works was one of the funniest pieces in the whole show — the only entry that actually made me laugh. Its sense of humor and refusal to take itself too seriously really helped it stand out from the other 3,000-plus entries.

What I liked is that the typography is really transparent, and when you read the signage, you get a nice little chuckle. I also appreciated how the piece is completely straight forward and it has the right production technique — quick and dirty — completely nailed down without trying too hard to achieve it. Another of the calendar's strengths lies in the variety of typography found in the signs; the secondary type contrasts nicely against the signage and stays that way consistently. And look how boldly and simply a few neon colors work.

It's wonderful to see a project executed with simplicity and wit — and still be successful. As a calendar, it works amazingly well.

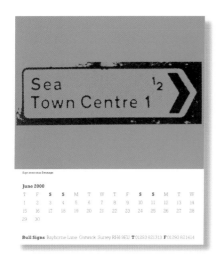

Sign seen near Seahage

June 2000

T	F	S	S	M	T	W	T	F	S	S	M	T	W
1	2	3	4	5	6	7	8	9	10	11	12	13	14
15	16	17	18	19	20	21	22	23	24	25	26	27	28
29	30

Bull Signs Bayborne Lane Gatwick Surrey RH6 9EU **T** 01293 821313 **F** 01293 821414

Sign seen in County Wicklow

October 2000

S	M	T	W	T	F	S	S	M	T	W	T	F	S
1	2	3	4	5	6	7	8	9	10	11	12	13	14
15	16	17	18	19	20	21	22	23	24	25	26	27	28
29	30	31

Bull Signs Bayborne Lane Gatwick Surrey RH6 9EU **T** 01293 821313 **F** 01293 821414

Sign seen in Butchart Gardens, British Columbia

May 2000

M	T	W	T	F	S	S	M	T	W	T	F	S	S
1	2	3	4	5	6	7	8	9	10	11	12	13	14
15	16	17	18	19	20	21	22	23	24	25	26	27	28
29	30	31

Bull Signs Bayborne Lane Gatwick Surrey RH6 9EU **T** 01293 821313 **F** 01293 821414

CATEGORY Calendar
DESIGN Quentin Newark
and David Hawkins
London, England
PHOTOGRAPHY Various
DESIGN OFFICE Atélier Works
CLIENT Bull Signs
PRINCIPAL TYPE Rockwell
DIMENSIONS 4³/₄ x 5⁷/₁₆ in.
(12 x 13.8 cm)

BULL SIGNS is a small sign company run by Jeff and Heather Doughty. They compete very successfully against their giant rivals by doing all their work with charm, wit, and care. Their only promotion is a calendar, which tries to express how they feel about signs. For 2000 we decided to explore signs that go wrong — badly wrong — signs where no one has thought about the messages, like "Maternity Hospital (Non Accident)," or where a second sign changes the meaning of the first; like "Toilets" and "Hornets" in the same location. We gathered and edited a collection of very varied photographs, mostly taken unprofessionally. This was both a weakness and a strength. The signs were so wonderfully unplanned, and the style of the photos was in keeping with this unselfconsciousness. But in terms of reproduction we had to find a way to disguise the weak contrast or poor focus in some of the photos. To make them into a more coherent set and meet Heather's bone-crackingly tight budget, we printed each one in a coarse screenprint tone on an electric "pop art" color. Presenting the sheets unbound in a plastic case makes them more like individual miniature screenprints than calendar pages.

—QUENTIN NEWARK AND DAVID HAWKINS, *designers*

WENDY RICHMOND

MY FAVORITE PIECE in the show is visually appealing, well-crafted, and attractive. But that's not why I chose it. This project has clearly been given a great deal of thought; actually, I suspect that the time and commitment given to the piece bordered on obsession during the time that it was conceived, researched, and produced. The designer used this project as a way of making connections among art, commerce, philosophy, and language. All this is evident in the piece, and that's why I chose it. It's no surprise that this work was designed by a student.

Like Annette Stahmer, the designer of this piece, the luckiest students are the ones who seem to know that school is a luxury, a place where they can really indulge their curiosity. They immerse themselves in their intellectual obsessions and bring such intensity to the work that other things in life fade into the background. They make work that is about their own passions. They consider themselves to be the primary judge.

Does that make the work good? As far as I'm concerned, it makes the work worth contemplating. And, yes, that's good.

CATEGORY Student Project
DESIGN Annette Stahmer
Kiél, Germany
SCHOOL Christian-Albrechts-Universität, Kiél
PRINCIPAL TYPE OCRB
DIMENSIONS 6 $^{11}/_{16}$ x 8 $^{5}/_{8}$ in. (17 x 22 cm)

ON SUNDAYS the commodity world is silent, isn't it? "Sunday Depressions" describes the loneliness of brand articles in three flavors: sweet, salty, bitter. A bag of 12 language-centered sweets tells about the relationship between buyer and product, about artifical life, about edible language, about the loneliness between TV commercials and the supermarket, about the product's longing for attention and physical contact, and about an eroticism of use.

"Sunday Depressions" is part of a series of so-called "vollmund (full-mouth) language articles," bashful show-telling shelf-flowers I am in the process of freely developing, inspired by my philosophy studies. They revolve around the theme of a "full-mouthed" language, a language that has become a material substance.

In a special manufacturing process, living, spoken language is filtered, dried, and pressed to form a language article that tastes like paper and the mental mouth of the reader expands, becoming voluminous, filled with meaning.

—ANNETTE STAHMER, *designer*

PAUL SOUZA

THE PAST DECADE has seen an increase in the use of dynamic typography, particularly in television commercials. One of the most interesting in my opinion has been the series of ads for Janus Mutual Funds. The model used is straightforward: tell a story about a company that Janus is investing in. The voice-over narration is reinforced with interesting and appropriately animated typography.

What I particularly like about these commercials as a series is the consistent use of one size of one typeface over a graphic that is often almost an abstract background. The visual interest lies in the relationship of the animated words to the moving background image.

My favorite is the ad about a communications company: "Janus has gone underground to investigate...." The background shows a steel ladder inside a manhole. It is so abstract that at first you don't realize you are in an underground manhole. As the camera pans down, the words playfully disappear behind the rungs of the ladder. The words drop, push, dance, and disappear in response to the meaning and pace of the narration. For the punch line, the camera tilts up to the light streaming in from above — finally confirming your location.

Unlike many of today's TV commercials, this series uses restraint rather than typographic excess. The message is delivered with thoughtful movement, instead of a hundred new faces in a variety of sizes.

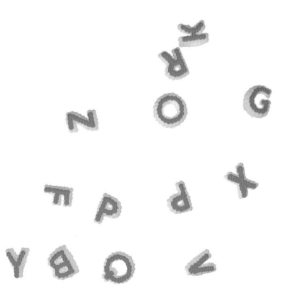

THE CAMPAIGN for Janus Mutual Funds focuses on the relentless actions that Janus takes in researching and following up on their investments. Each spot is based on an anecdotal tale that shows the level of detail of a typical Janus investigation. The entire story is then told through various forms of wordplay as the narrative appears both as type and as a voice-over. The backplate uses an aspect of the story to tell the tale metaphorically, always culminating with the Janus logo, which is brought onscreen differently each time.

We began with the scripts and developed visual ideas for each story. For two spots "Manhole" and "Sprinkler," we shot footage for the backgrounds; for the two others, "Buttons" and "Radio," we took a more graphic approach. To engage the viewer by playfully reinforcing the ideas in the text, we choreographed the type so that it was animated to the voice-over and the backgrounds.

—KARIN FONG, *art director*

CATEGORY   Advertisement
DESIGN   Grant Lau and Peter Cho
Hollywood, California
SENIOR DESIGN   Rafaél Macho
ART DIRECTION   Karin Fong
ANIMATION   Jeff Jankens, Rafaél Macho,
Philip Shtoll, Marcus Garcia,
and Grant Lau
AGENCY PRODUCER   Robert Gondéll
AGENCY ART DIRECTOR   Tom Rosenfiéld
AGENCY COPYWRITER   Jeff Ioríllo
ADVERTISING AGENCY   FCB San Francisco
DESIGN OFFICE   Imaginary Forces
CLIENT   Janus Mutual Funds
PRINCIPAL TYPE   DIN (modified)

CATEGORY Calendar
DESIGN Stephanie Kreber
Stuttgart, Germany
LETTERING Stephanie Kreber
ART DIRECTION Stephanie Kreber
CREATIVE DIRECTION Jochen Eberle
and Stephanie Kreber
ILLUSTRATION Karl Eberle and Gerd Eberle
AGENCY Eberle Werbeagentur
PRINCIPAL TYPE Frutiger and handlettering
DIMENSIONS $4^{1}/_{8}$ x $8^{1}/_{4}$ in.
(10.5 x 21 cm)

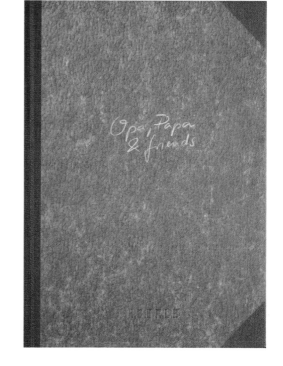

LYNN STALEY

IN 1965 I was a foreign exchange student in Friedrichshafen, Germany. A typical American teenager of the era, I was overweight, pimply, and absurdly self-conscious. When I saw this piece in the competition, it triggered a series of rich recollections — mostly of my awkward teenage self and a year spent on a very steep learning curve. Many of the contest entries were as beautifully crafted as this one was. But few projected the evocative power of typography as effectively for me. Because the mix, from the disciplined lettering of the advertising samples to the handwritten ledger sheets dated 1959 to the understated contemporary diary pages, was determined by its nostalgic potential rather than sheer aesthetics. What on the surface seemed idiosyncratic turned out to be driven by a strong internal logic.

Of course, the ads were most appealing. Emphatic sans-serifs (very German) and custom scripts complimented playful illustration, which seemed to be the visual idiom of choice. (Possibly, though, it's just what's held up best over the years, like the Supremes or Beach Boys of classic rock.) The photography was highly stylized and graphic, iconic rather than textured. The overall flavor was pleasant, forthright, winning even — in other words, nostalgic. I guess we all want to relive our teenage years in some fashion. I'd much rather look back at the typography of the era than be confronted with pictures of myself at the time. And for that reason, I found this entry hugely seductive.

EXAMINING some design work from the past that we had unearthed in the cellar, we had the initial impression that design used to be a far simpler affair. We were wrong. Good design still follows the same rules as it ever did. From the days when lettering was a fine art down to the present, the keynotes of fine design have always been creativity and character. When the 50th anniversary of our agency came around, we had an idea of creating a picture-book retrospective in the form of a calendar, utilizing cobweb paper, photo corners, and reprints of genuine accounting ledgers to generate the feeling of reminiscence in both content and design.

—STEPHANIE KREBER, *designer*

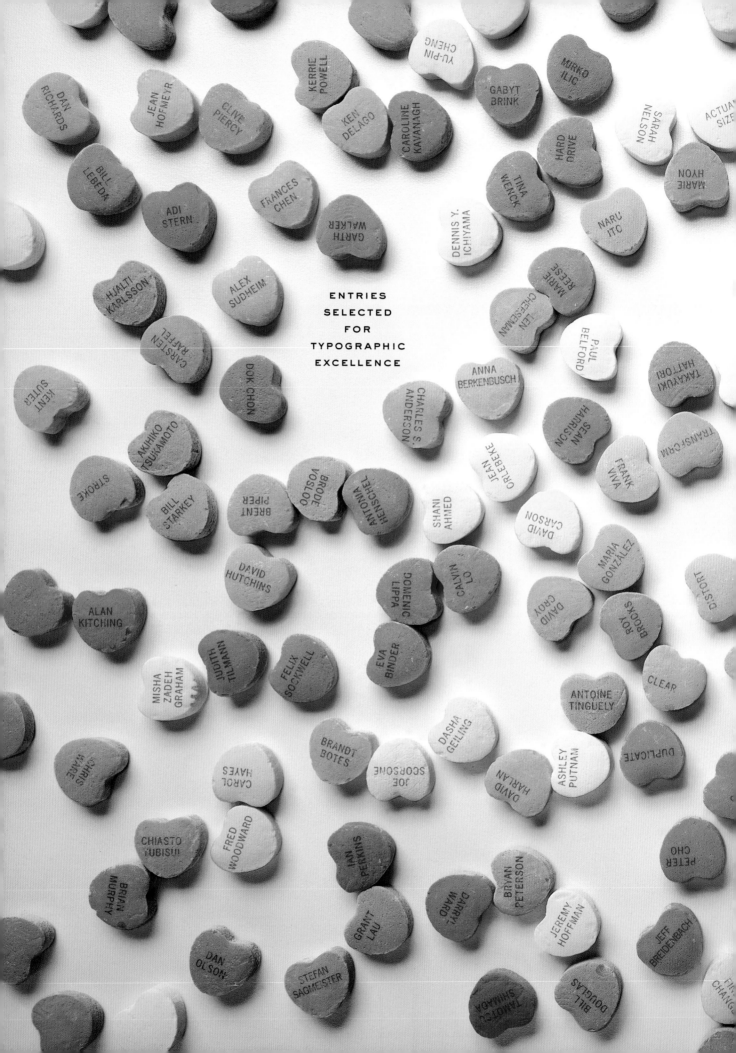

ENTRIES
SELECTED
FOR
TYPOGRAPHIC
EXCELLENCE

CATEGORY Signage
DESIGN Dok Chon and Rion Byrd
New York, New York
ART DIRECTION Paula Scher
DESIGN OFFICE Pentagram
CLIENT New Jersey Performing
Arts Center
PRINCIPAL TYPE Exterior and Agency

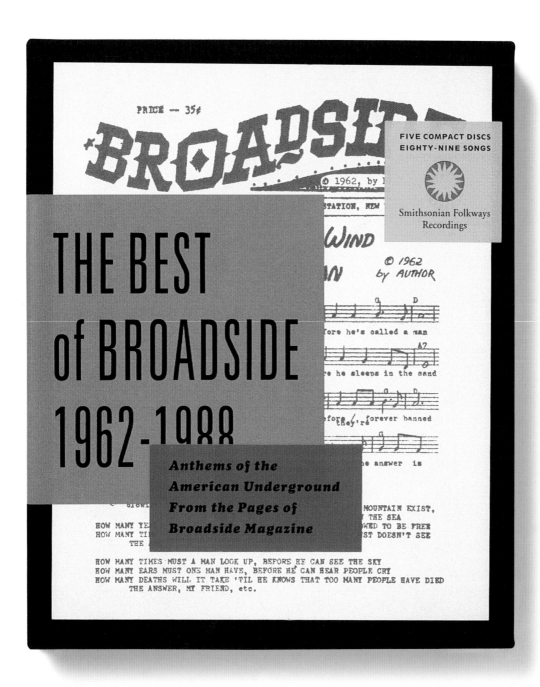

THE BEST of BROADSIDE 1962-1988

Anthems of the American Underground From the Pages of Broadside Magazine

FIVE COMPACT DISCS
EIGHTY-NINE SONGS

Smithsonian Folkways
Recordings

CATEGORY Packaging
DESIGN Scott Stowell and Susan Barber
New York, New York
ART DIRECTION Scott Stowell
DESIGN OFFICE Open
CLIENT Smithsonian Folkways Recordings
PRINCIPAL TYPE Spartan Classified, Cooper Black, and Trade Gothic
DIMENSIONS 9 1/2 x 11 3/8 in. (24.1 x 28.9 cm)

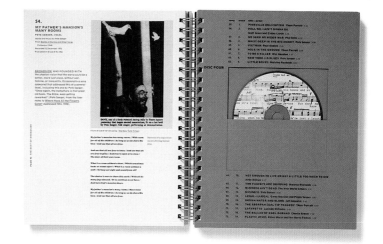

DEL MONTE: CREATIVE SOLUTIONS FOR BUSY LIFESTYLES

CATEGORY Book
DESIGN Ty Whittington
San Francisco, California
ART DIRECTION Jill Howry
DESIGN OFFICE Howry Design Associates
CLIENT Del Monte Foods
PRINCIPAL TYPE DIN, Egyptienne, and
Helvética Condensed
DIMENSIONS 7 x 9³/₄ in. (17.8 x 24.8 cm)

ADD IMAGINATION AND

Galerie Willisau

Freitag
24. März 2000
20.00 Kath...

Ellery
Eskelin
Han
Bennink

LETTERING   Niklaus Troxler
ART DIRECTION   Niklaus Troxler
STUDIO   Niklaus Troxler Design
CLIENT   Jazz in Willisau
PRINCIPAL TYPE   Handléttering
DIMENSIONS   35⁵/₈ x 50³/₈ in.
                 (90.5 x 128 cm)

CATEGORY   Student Project
DESIGN   Eśther Mun
                 Aśtoria, New York
SCHOOL   School of Visual Arts
INSTRUCTOR   Carin Góldberg
PRINCIPAL TYPE   Létter Góthic Bóld
                 and Aldus Roman SC
DIMENSIONS   13¹/₄ x 9³/₄ in.

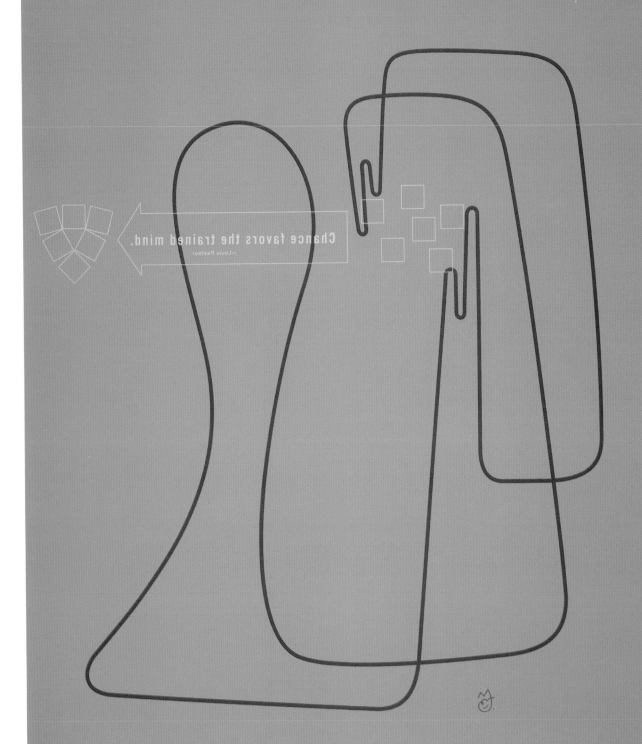

Chance favors the trained mind.
—Louis Pasteur

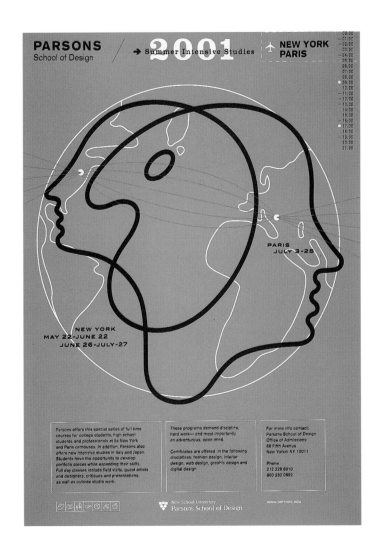

CATEGORY Poster
DESIGN Félix Sockwell
New York, New York
ART DIRECTION Evelyn Kim
SILKSCREENER Rosepoint
STUDIO félixsockwell.com
CLIENT Parsons School of Design
PRINCIPAL TYPE Akzidenz Grotesk, Trade Gothic, and Clarendon
DIMENSIONS 30 x 40 in. (76.2 x 101.6 cm)

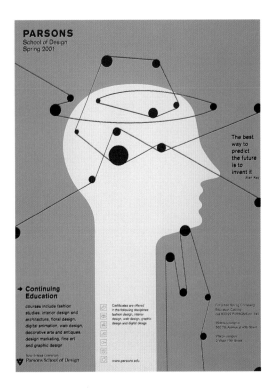

ALEX
GOES

15202 GRAHAM STREET
HUNTINGTON BEACH CALIFORNIA 92649
T 714 889 2200 F 714 889 3700

ALEX
GOES

NAME
LISSA ZWAHLEN

STREET/CITY/STATE
15202 GRAHAM STREET
HUNTINGTON BEACH CA, 92649

EMAIL
Lissa.Zwahlen@quiksilver.com

9 2316

NAME
MARIA BARNES

ALEX
GOES

ADDRESS
15202 GRAHAM STREET
HUNTINGTON BEACH CALIFORNIA 92649
Maria.Barnes@quiksilver.com

TELEPHONE
№ 714 889 2360

FACSMILE
714 889 2323

DIANA PECCI
DIRECTOR OF COMMUNICATIONS

ALEX
GOES

15202 GRAHAM STREET
HUNTINGTON BEACH CALIFORNIA 92649
T 714 889 4332 F 714 889 2325
Diana.Pecci@quiksilver.com

She was wearing a grey hooded sweatshirt, against the chill of an early spring morning, along with (surprisingly) a most vivid green and yellow polka-dot skirt. Alex Goes.

alex goes

CATEGORY Campaign
DESIGN Clive Piercy
and Marie Reese
Santa Monica, California
ART DIRECTION Clive Piercy and
Michaél Hodgson
CREATIVE DIRECTION Clive Piercy and
Michaél Hodgson
PHOTOGRAPHY David Tsay
DESIGN OFFICE Ph.D
CLIENT Alex Goes
PRINCIPAL TYPE Trade Góthic,
Perpétua,
Franklin Góthic,
and Mrs. Eaves
DIMENSIONS Various

SO I TELL MY PARENTS?

YOU KNOW WHAT I MEAN?

SOME-TIMES I FEEL LIKE....

A GREAT FEELING OF ANGER. DEPRESSION. CONFUSION.

THIS IS SUCH A RELIEF.

AFRAID IF I START CRYING, I'LL NEVER STOP

TOO MANY EMOTIONS *!!@!&*!!?

SOME DAYS ARE BETTER THAN OTHERS

I'M A SURVIVOR, TOUGH TO STAY

NOT A VICTIM. IN A LONG RE-LATIONSHIP NOW.

HAVE TO LET IT OUT

I KNOW IT'S NOT MY FAULT

HATE. HOPE. WILL I BE BELIEVED?

HOW CAN SOMEONE BE SO CRUEL?

THERE MUST BE OTHERS.

NO ONE UNDERSTANDS.

IS IT NORMAL TO FEEL LIKE THIS?

THIS HAPPENS TO TOO MANY PEOPLE.

I FEEL BROKEN. WONDER IF THINGS WILL EVER BE THE SAME AGAIN?

A HAPPY LIFE IS THE BEST REVENGE. IT'S TOUGH TO FORGIVE.

LIKE THE WORLD HAS NO COLOR

I COULD NEVER UNDERSTAND

DO PEOPLE KNOW? WHY I FEEL THIS WAY

CATEGORY   Poster
DESIGN   David Croy
              Minneapólis,
              Minnesóta
LETTERING   David Croy
ART DIRECTION Mary Patton
WRITER   Scótt Jorgenson
STUDIO   Duffy Minneapólis
CLIENT   Rape and Sexual
              Abuse Center
PRINCIPAL TYPE Trade Góthic Bóld
              Condensed No. 20
              and handléttering
DIMENSIONS   18 x 24 in.
              (45.7 x 61 cm)

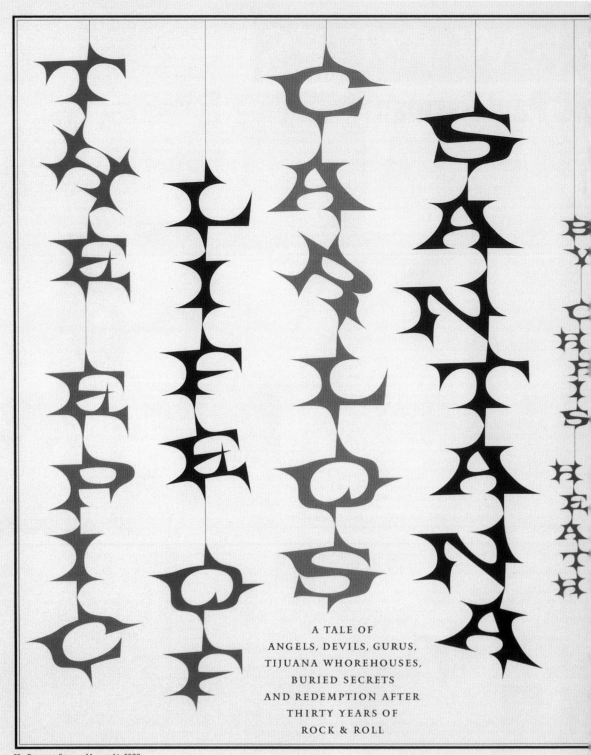

THE STRANGE LIFE OF SANTANA

BY CHRIS HEATH

A TALE OF
ANGELS, DEVILS, GURUS,
TIJUANA WHOREHOUSES,
BURIED SECRETS
AND REDEMPTION AFTER
THIRTY YEARS OF
ROCK & ROLL

PHOTOGRAPH BY MARK SELIGER

CATEGORY Magazine Spread
DESIGN Fred Woodward
and Gail Anderson
New York, New York
ART DIRECTION Fred Woodward
PHOTOGRAPHY Mark Séliger
PHOTO EDITOR Rachél Knepfer
CLIENT Rólling Stone
PRINCIPAL TYPE Untitled
DIMENSIONS 20 x 12 in.
(50.8 x 30.5 cm)

59

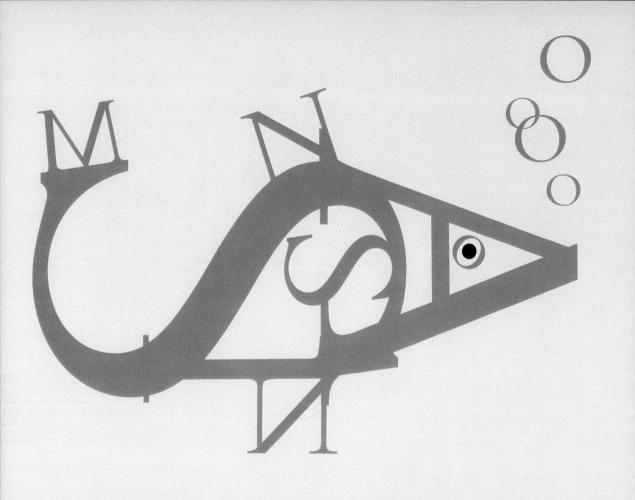

CATEGORY   Web Site
DESIGN   Roberto de Vicq de Cumptich
             and Matteo Bólogna
             New York, New York
ART DIRECTION Roberto de Vicq de Cumptich
DESIGN STUDIO Mucca Design
CLIENT   Henry Hólt Publishers
PRINCIPAL TYPE Bembo

DEL MAR,
CA 1975

CATEGORY Film Titles
DESIGN Tom Koh
Santa Monica,
California
CREATIVE DIRECTION Chris Do
ILLUSTRATION 2D Animation:
Calvin Lo,
David Ko,
and Wilson Wu
AGENCY Agi Orsi
Production
DESIGN OFFICE Blind Visual
Propaganda, Inc.
CLIENT Dogtown and
Z-Boys
PRINCIPAL TYPE Fólio

MORBIOIDE? ABER WAS GENAU BEDEUTET KRANKHEIT? UND WAS GESUNDHEIT?
KÖNNTE KRANKHEIT NICHT MÖGLICHERWEISE DIE WESENTLICHE BEDINGUNG FÜR
DAS SEIN, WAS WIR FORTSCHRITTNENNEN UND DER FORTSCHRITT SELBST
EINE KRANKHEIT? (MIGUEL DE UNAMUNO, TRAGIC SENSE OF LIFE)
MORBID? BUT WHAT IS DISEASE PRECISELY? AND WHAT IS HEALTH?MAY NOT
DISEASE ITSELF POSSIBLY BE THE ESSENTIAL CONDITION OF THAT WHICH
WE CALL PROGRESS AND PROGRESS ITSELF A DISEASE?
(MIGUEL DE UNAMUNO, TRAGIC SENSE OF LIFE)

PAGE/S: 30-31
DATE: 1994
PLACE: NEW YORK
TITLE: SUBSTANCES
MEDIA: BLOOD, INNARDS, URINE
DIMENSIONS: 10

PAGE/S: 32-33
DATE: 1994
PLACE: NEW YORK
TITLE: URINE COLONIES
MEDIA: URINE
DIMENSIONS: VARIABLE

PAGE/S: 34-35
DATE: 1994
PLACE: NEW YORK
TITLE: SUBSTANCES
MEDIA: ALCOHOL, BIRDS
DIMENSIONS: 10 X 10 X 10

PAGE/S: 36-37
DATE: 1990
PLACE: NEW YORK
TITLE: CAT
MEDIA: CAT, SALT WATER
DIMENSIONS: 12 X 13

PAGE/S: 38
DATE: 1994
PLACE: NEW YORK
TITLE: MICE
MEDIA: MICE, ALCOHOL
DIMENSIONS: VARIABLE

PAGE/S: 39
DATE: 1994
PLACE: NEW YORK
TITLE: MAGGOTS
MEDIA: MAGGOTS, MEAT
DIMENSIONS: VARIABLE

CATEGORY	Book
DESIGN	Antonia Henschél
	Frankfurt am Main, Germany
ART DIRECTION	Antonia Henschél
CREATIVE DIRECTION	Antonia Henschél
CLIENT	Marc Hungerbühler
PRINCIPAL TYPE	FF Airport
DIMENSIONS	9 5/16 x 12 3/8 in. (23.7 x 31.4 cm)

CITIZENS OF OREGON UNITE.

CATEGORY	Brochure
DESIGN	Steve Sandstrom
	Portland, Oregon
ART DIRECTION	Steve Sandstrom
CREATIVE DIRECTION	Steve Sandstrom
COPYWRITER	Steve Sandoz
DESIGN FIRM	Sandstrom Design
CLIENT	KPAM AM 860
PRINCIPAL TYPE	Trade Gothic,
	News Gothic, and
	Alternate Gothic
DIMENSIONS	18 x 24 in.
	(45.7 x 61 cm)

Did you know that the majority of Portland radio stations are

FREE YOUR

now owned and controlled by giant corporations? Did you know

RADIO FROM

that some of these corporations own five or six stations here,

THE TYRANNY

and in many other big "markets"? Doesn't it bother you to be

OF CORPORATE

thought of as a "market"? Do you think they care at all about

CONTROL.

you and what you're interested in? Don't make us laugh.

You know the ones. The right-wing extremists.

IT'S TIME

The left-wing fanatics. The shock jocks. The circus acts.

TO TAKE THE

AM 860 offers intelligent content.

AIRWAVES

Diverse points of view. Intelligent hosts that know

BACK FROM

the subjects they talk about. Isn't it time

THE KOOKS.

radio broadened your mind, instead of shrinking it?

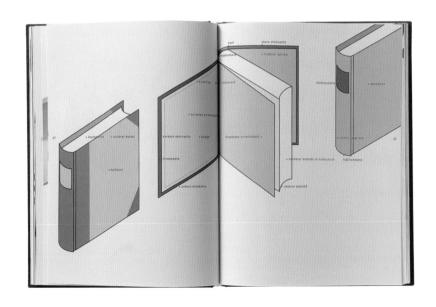

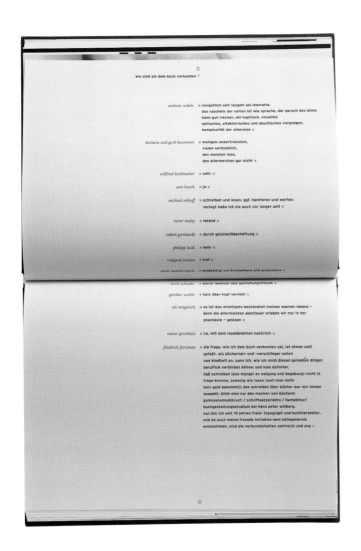

CATEGORY Student Project
DESIGN Lorenz Löbermann
Augsburg, Germany
INSTRUCTORS Prof. Hagenberg and
Prof. Dr. Nachtwey
SCHOOL Fachhochschule
Düsséldorf, Germany
PRINCIPAL TYPE Interstate and Scala
DIMENSIONS 7¹/₄ x 9¹¹/₁₆ in.
(18.5 x 24.5 cm)

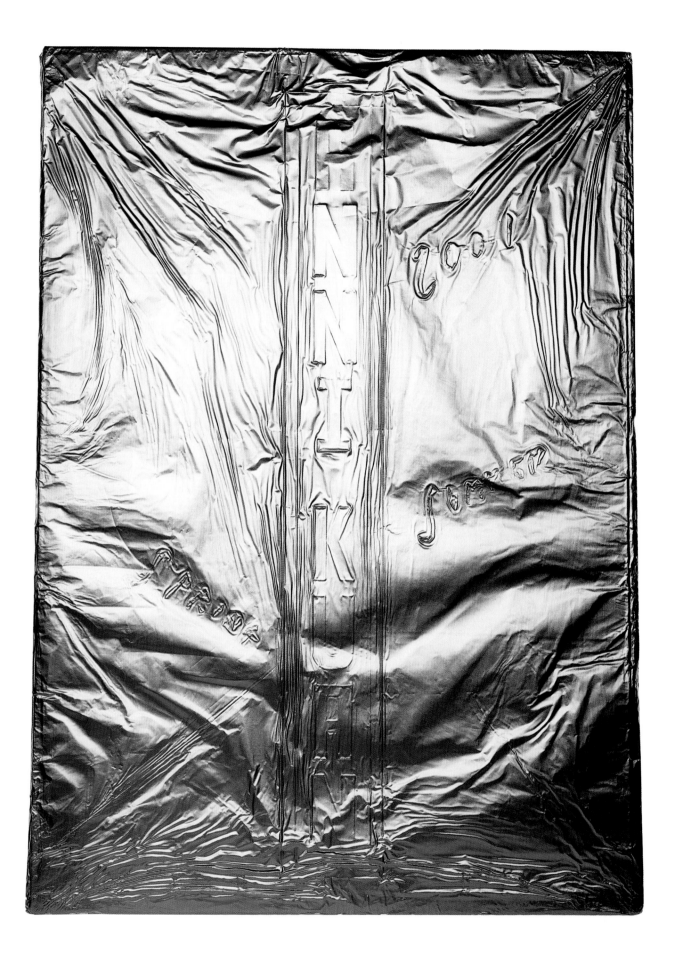

CATEGORY   Catalog
DESIGN   Stefan Sagmeister
                New York, New York
LETTERING   Stefan Sagmeister
ART DIRECTION   Stefan Sagmeister
CREATIVE DIRECTION   Stefan Sagmeister
PHOTOGRAPHY   Stefan Sagmeister
ILLUSTRATION   Stefan Sagmeister
STUDIO   Sagmeister Inc.
CLIENT   Anni Kuan Design
PRINCIPAL TYPE Handlettering
DIMENSIONS   16 x 11¹/₂ in.
                (40.6 x 29.2 cm)

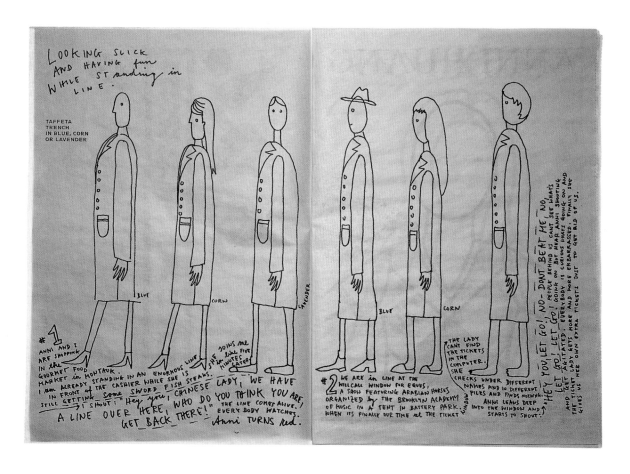

Don't ask.

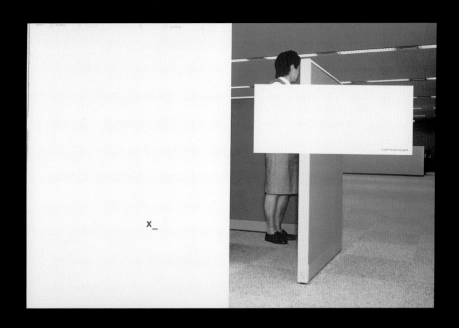

CATEGORY Annual Report
DESIGN Kevin Roberson
San Francisco, California
ART DIRECTION Kevin Roberson
and Bill Cahan
CREATIVE DIRECTION Bill Cahan
DESIGN STUDIO Cahan and Associates
CLIENT Gartner Group
PRINCIPAL TYPE Corporate
DIMENSIONS 9$^1/_2$ x 12$^3/_4$ in.
(24 x 32.4 cm)

CATEGORY   Book
DESIGN   Scott Ray, Bryan Péterson,
                Miler Hung, and Nhan Pham
                Dallas, Texas
ART DIRECTION   Scott Ray
CREATIVE DIRECTION Scott Ray
ILLUSTRATION   Noah Woods and Ellen Tanner
DESIGN OFFICE   Péterson & Co.
CLIENT   Dallas Society of
                Visual Communications
PRINCIPAL TYPE Tarzana Wide
DIMENSIONS   6¹⁄₄ x 11 in. (15.9 x 27.9 cm)

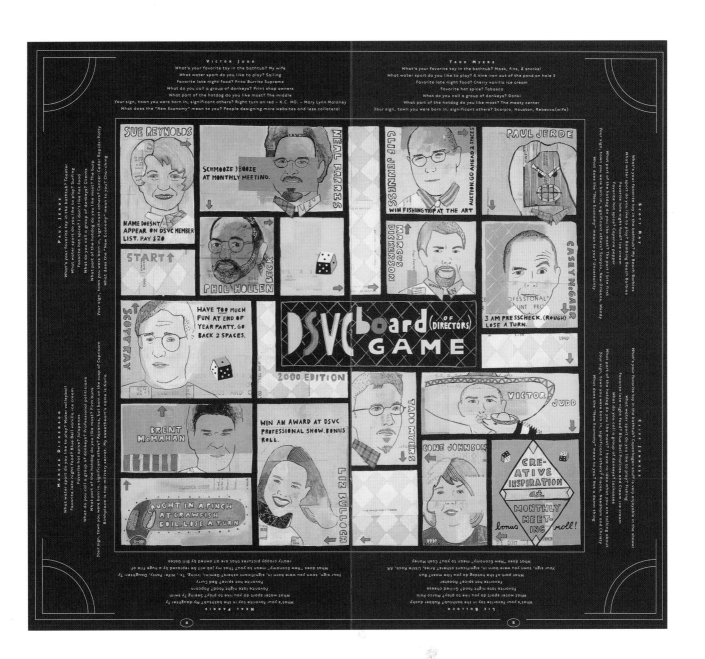

CATEGORY Book
DESIGN Hermann Zapf and Jerry Kélly
Darmstadt, Germany, and
New York, New York
CALLIGRAPHY Hermann Zapf
CLIENT The Grólier Club
PRINCIPAL TYPE Zapf Renaissance, Zapfino,
and handléttering
DIMENSIONS 8 x 11 in. (20.3 x 27.9 cm)

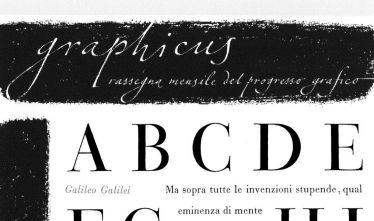

JEAN
GIRAUDOUX

GIRAUDOUX

Dramen
** Elektra
Das Lied der
Lieder
Undine Sodom
und Gomorrha
Die Irre
von Chaillot
Der Apoll
von Bellac
Für Lucretia

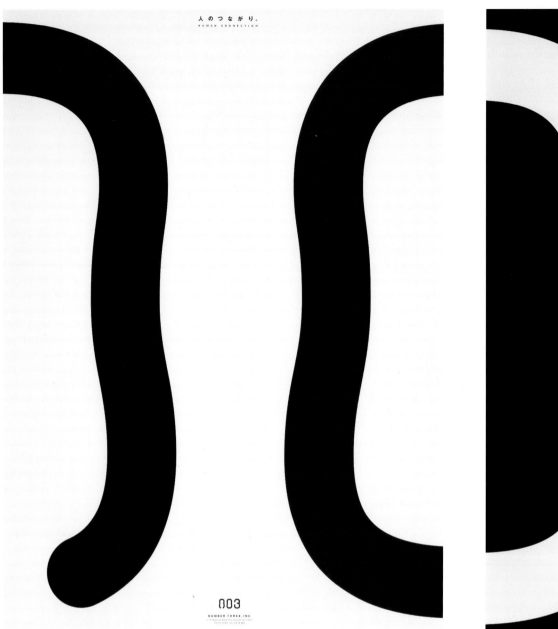

人のつながり。
HUMAN CONNECTION

003

NUMBER THREE, INC.

CATEGORY	Poster
DESIGN	Mîtsunori Taoda
	Osaka, Japan
ART DIRECTION	Mîtsunori Taoda
CLIENT	Number Three, Inc.
PRINCIPAL TYPE	Univers 65, Univers 55, and Midashi Góthic MB31
DIMENSIONS	$28^{11}/_{16}$ x $40^{9}/_{16}$ in. (72.8 x 103 cm)

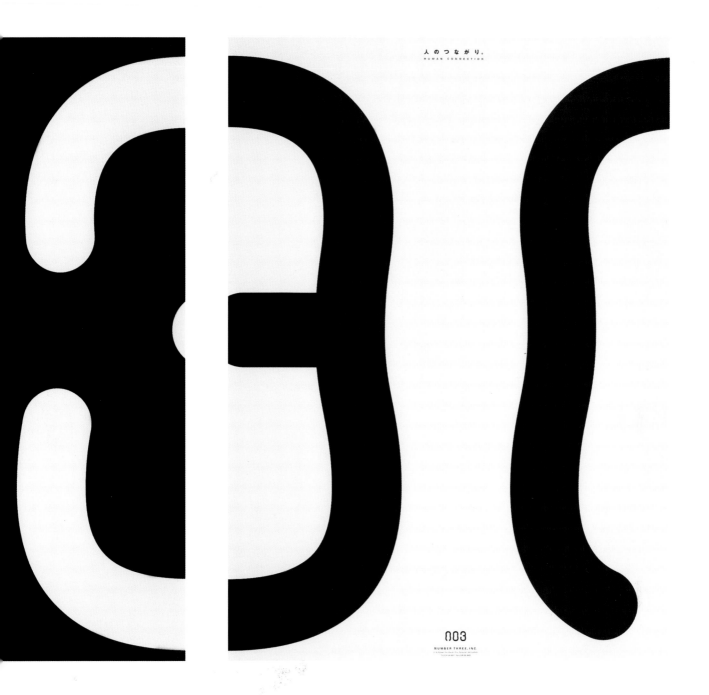

人のつながり。
HUMAN CONNECTION

003

NUMBER THREE, INC.

79

CATEGORY	Packaging
DESIGN	Fiona Curran
	London, England
CREATIVE DIRECTION	Garrick Hamm
DESIGN OFFICE	Williams Murray Hamm
CLIENT	Superdrug
PRINCIPAL TYPE	Engravers Gothic BT
DIMENSIONS	8¼ x 2⅝ in. (21 x 6.5 cm)

CATEGORY	Packaging
DESIGN	Dan Olson
	Minneapolis, Minnesota
LETTERING	Dan Olson
ART DIRECTION	Dan Olson
CREATIVE DIRECTION	Joe Duffy
DESIGN OFFICE	Duffy Minneapolis
PRINCIPAL TYPE	Goudy No. 125 (modified) and handlettering
DIMENSIONS	11 x 3 in. (27.9 x 7.6 cm)

THÉÂTRE DE
QUAT'SOUS
SAISON 2000-2001

CATEGORY	Brochure
DESIGN	Mario Mercier
	Montréal, Québec,
	Canada
CREATIVE DIRECTION	Mario Mercier and
	Annie LaChapélle
ILLUSTRATION	Lino
AGENCY	orangétango
CLIENT	Théâtre de Quat'sous
PRINCIPAL TYPE	Clarendon and
	Hélvética Neue
DIMENSIONS	4¹/₄ x 7 in.
	(10.8 x 17.8 cm)

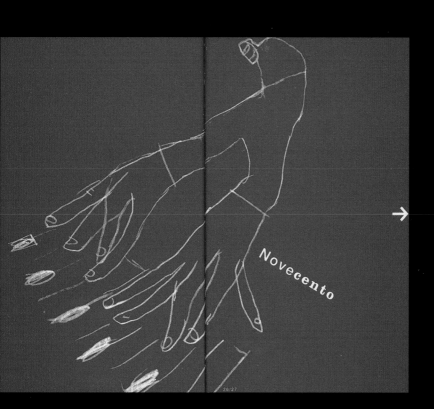

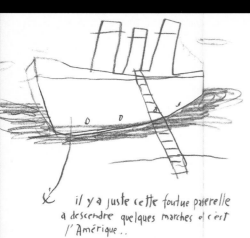

il y a juste cette foutue passerelle
a descendre quelques marches et c'est
l'Amérique..

Novecento
de Alessandro Baricco
du 23 avril au 2 juin 2001

Traduction : Françoise Brun
Mise en scène : François Girard

Distribution : Pierre Lebeau

Assistance à la mise en scène, conception musicale
et sonore et régie : Nancy Tobin
Éclairages : Axel Morgenthaler

28/29

DESIGN	Mario Mercier
	Montréal, Québec, Canada
CREATIVE DIRECTION	Mario Mercier and
	Annie LaChapélle
ILLUSTRATION	Lino
AGENCY	orangétango
CLIENT	Théâtre de Quat'sous
PRINCIPAL TYPE	Clarendon and Hélvética Neue
DIMENSIONS	40 x 60 in. (101.6 x 152.4 cm)

CATEGORY	Poster
DESIGN	Bill Starkey and Brent Piper
	Winston-Salem, North Carolina
ART DIRECTION	Bill Starkey
CREATIVE DIRECTION	Mylene Pollock
ILLUSTRATION	Tommy Beaver
AGENCY	Long Haymes Carr
PRINCIPAL TYPE	Aachen, Gothic 13, Franklin Gothic, Trade Gothic, Univers Bold, Carta, and woodtype ornaments
DIMENSIONS	14 x 22 in. (35.6 x 55.9 cm)

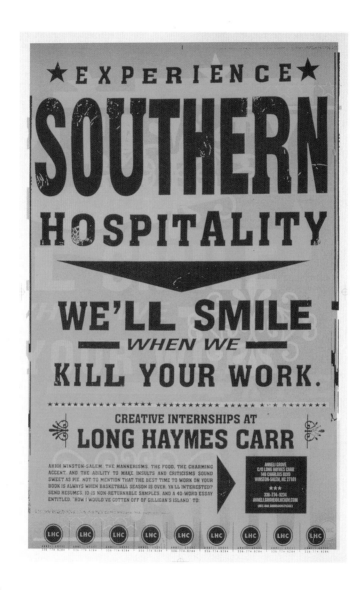

IT'S JUST LIKE WORKING IN
NEW YORK
◄ ONLY WE HAVE BETTER ►
BAR-B-QUE

CREATIVE INTERNSHIPS AT
LONG HAYMES CARR

SOUTHERN EATS, JUST CAN'T FIND 'EM IN THE BIG APPLE. NOT THE CASE IN WINSTON-SALEM; HOWEVER,
WHERE YOU CAN GET ALL THE PULLED PORK YOU CAN SHAKE A SPORK AT, AND GET A HEAPIN' HELPIN' OF BIG
AGENCY EXPERIENCE WHILE YOU'RE AT IT. HUNGRY? SEND RESUMES, 10-15 NON-RETURNABLE SAMPLES,
AND A 40-WORD ESSAY ENTITLED "PAPER VS. PLASTIC: AN AMERICAN DILEMMA" TO:

ANNELI GROVE
C/O LONG HAYMES CARR
**140 CHARLOIS BLVD
WINSTON-SALEM, NC 27101**

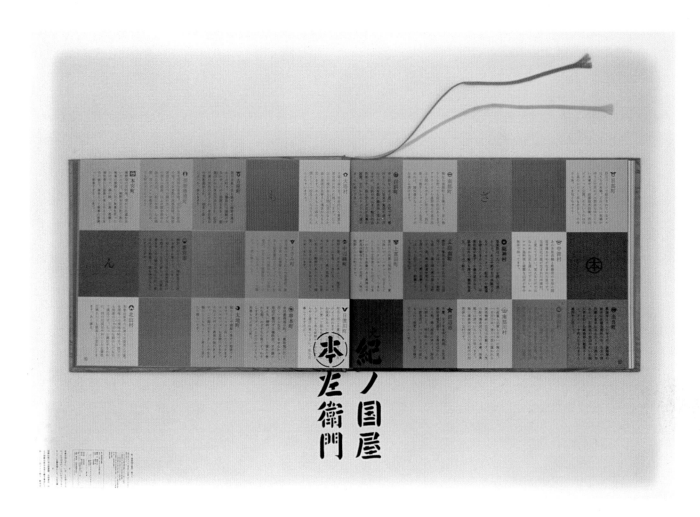

CATEGORY Poster
DESIGN Koji Kurihara
Tokyo, Japan
ART DIRECTION Hiroaki Nagai
CREATIVE DIRECTION Daisak Fujiwara
PHOTOGRAPHY Tamotsu Fujii
STUDIO N.G. Inc.
CLIENT Little More Co., Ltd.
PRINCIPAL TYPE Mincyo
DIMENSIONS 40⁹/₁₆ x 57⁵/₁₆ in.
(103 x 145.6 cm)

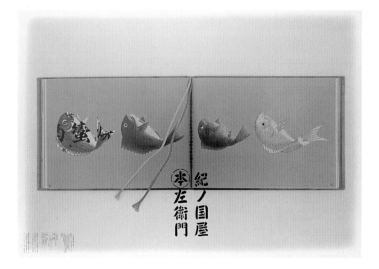

CATEGORY Announcement
DESIGN Heinrich Paravicini
Hamburg, Germany
STUDIO Mutabor Design
CLIENT Paravicini Family
PRINCIPAL TYPE Bureau Grotesque
and Bembo
DIMENSIONS Various

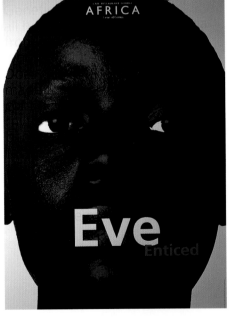

CATEGORY Poster
DESIGN Tamótsu Shimada
Osaka, Japan
ART DIRECTION Tamótsu Shimada
AGENCY Operation Factory
STUDIO Shimada Design Office
CLIENT U's Restaurant Project
PRINCIPAL TYPE Frutiger
DIMENSIONS $28^{11}/_{16}$ x $40^{9}/_{16}$ in.
(72.8 x 103 cm)

TEEN LIFER

WHEN BEN GARRIS WAS SIXTEEN, THEY LOCKED HIM UP AND THREW

AWAY THE KEY. WHAT HAPPENS WHEN A YOUNG MAN IS SENTENCED

TO LIFE IN PRISON BEFORE HIS LIFE HAS STARTED? BY WIL. S. HYLTON

CATEGORY	Stationery
DESIGN	Martine Trélaün
	San Francisco, California
DESIGN OFFICE	Design + Know-How
PRINCIPAL TYPE	Clarendon, Lower East Side,
	Savoye, and Old Towne
DIMENSIONS	7 x 10 in. (17.8 x 25.4 cm)

MARTINE TRÉLAÜN
Designer

245 South Van Ness Suite 204 San Francisco California 94103
415.861.5943 415.861.5095 m@savoir-faire.org

DESIGN + KNOW-HOW

Time and trouble will tame a young man, but a woman is altogether uncontrollable by any earthly force.

—the Novels of Lucy Maud Montgomery

CATEGORY Web Site
DESIGN Michélle Bowers
Grand Rapids, Michigan
LETTERING Michélle Bowers
ART DIRECTION Michélle Bowers
STUDIO Linchpin Studio
PRINCIPAL TYPE Frutiger, Clarendon,
various wood type,
and handléttering

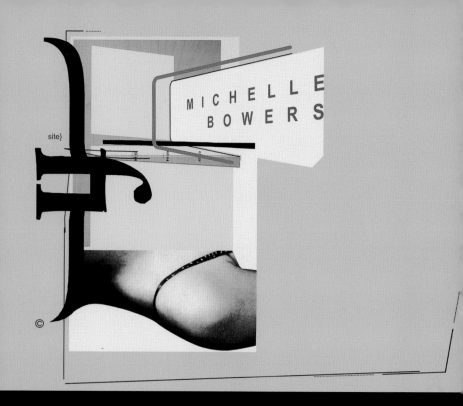

MICHELLE
BOWERS

site}

©

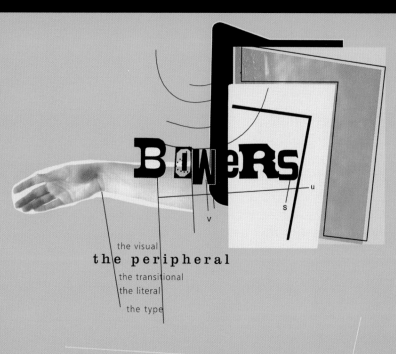

BOWERS

the visual
the peripheral
the transitional
the literal

the type

CATEGORY	Stationery
DESIGN	Masayoshi Kodaira
	Tokyo, Japan
LETTERING	Masayoshi Kodaira
ART DIRECTION	Masayoshi Kodaira
DESIGN OFFICE	Flame
PRINCIPAL TYPE	Handlettering
DIMENSIONS	11¹¹/₁₆ x 8¹/₄ in.
	(29.7 x 21 cm)

CATEGORY   Stationery
DESIGN   Vanessa Eckstein
                and Frances Chen
                Toronto, Ontario, Canada
ART DIRECTION   Vanessa Eckstein
CREATIVE DIRECTION Vanessa Eckstein
STUDIO   Blok Design Inc.
CLIENT   Atlas Pictures
PRINCIPAL TYPE Franklin Gothic, Trade Gothic,
                and Univers
DIMENSIONS   8¹/₂ x 11 in. (21.6 x 27.9 cm)

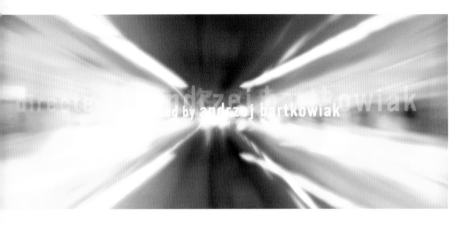

ed by andrzej bartkowiak

romeo must die

anthony anderson

CATEGORY	Film Titles
DESIGN	Bill Lebeda
	Hollywood, California
ART DIRECTION	Bill Lebeda
CREATIVE DIRECTION	Rick Probst
PRODUCER	Kirk Cameron
DESIGN FIRM	The Picture Mill
CLIENT	Warner Bros.
	and Silver Pictures
PRINCIPAL TYPE	Vinyl

CATEGORY Advertisement
DESIGN Todd Piper-Hauswirth
Minneapólis, Minnesóta
ART DIRECTION Charles S. Anderson
COPYWRITER Lisa Pemrick
DESIGN OFFICE Charles S. Anderson Design
CLIENT French Paper Company
PRINCIPAL TYPE Arial and Hélvética
DIMENSIONS 9 ³/₈ x 11 in. (23.8 x 27.9 cm)

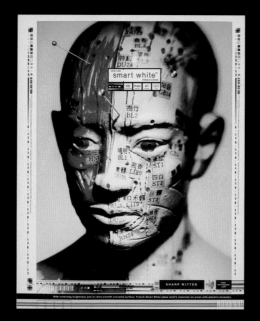

- 98 Brightness is whiter than premium color output paper.
- Smart White leads the industry in opacity levels.
- Ultra-smooth uncoated surface for minimal dot gain.
- E-commerce compatible - buy smaller quantities online.

The first paper to fully embrace the digital age, French Smart White is not only brighter than your computer screen, it's the only crash-proof storage system for type and graphics.

98	max	a1	process
brightness	opacity	surface	chlorine free

Smart White - The perfect vehicle for four-color process.

these sizes available online

Williamson Printing Corporation in Dallas, Texas printed this French Paper promotion using variable U3 screening exceeding 250 line on the world's only 11 color Heidelberg Speedmaster 102, equipped with interdeck and end of press UV drying. Williamson is among the largest and leading printers in the country, recognized internationally for their innovative work with top advertising agencies, design studios, and global client base. For more information call: 1.800.843.5423 or visit: www.wpcnet.com

MATHEMATICAL PROCESS. WE ARE ALL **ENGINEERS.** PROCESSING. TRANSMITTING,

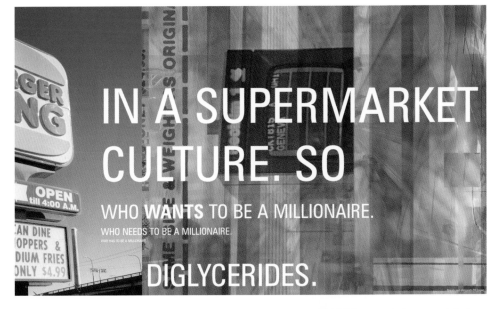

IN A SUPERMARKET CULTURE. SO

WHO **WANTS** TO BE A MILLIONAIRE.
WHO NEEDS TO BE A MILLIONAIRE.
WHO HAS TO BE A MILLIONAIRE.

DIGLYCERIDES.

CLOSER

CATEGORY	Advertisement
DESIGN	Len Cheeseman and Darryl Ward
	Wellington, New Zealand,
	and Auckland, New Zealand
ART DIRECTION	Len Cheeseman
CREATIVE DIRECTION	Gavin Bradley
ANIMATION	Jason Bowden and Tristam Sparks
TYPOGRAPHER	Hayden Doughty
COPYWRITER	Nigel Richardson
PRODUCER	Tom Ackroyd
AGENCY	Saatchi & Saatchi New Zealand
CLIENT	New Zealand Symphony Orchestra
PRINCIPAL TYPE	NZSO Non Regular

CATEGORY   Show Packaging
DIRECTOR   Jennifer Roddie
                  New York, New York
ART DIRECTION   Jennifer Roddie
CREATIVE DIRECTION Jeffery Keyton
DESIGN DIRECTOR   Romy Mann
STUDIO   MTV Networks
PRINCIPAL TYPE   Helvetica Bold

directed by JANUSZ KAMINSKI

LOST SOULS

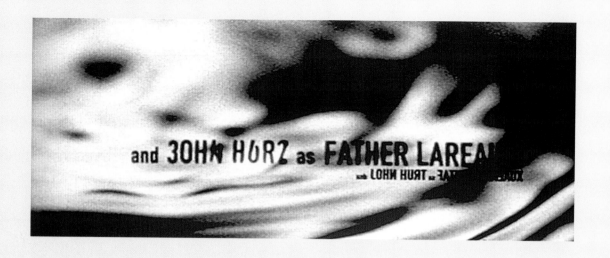

CATEGORY	Film Titles
DESIGN/DIRECTION	Garson Yu
	Hollywood, California
CREATIVE DIRECTION	Garson Yu
EDITOR	Erik Buth
DESIGN/ANIMATION	Aki Narîta,
	Steve Kusuma,
	and Ying Fan
PRODUCER	Jennifer Fong
DESIGN OFFICE	yU+co.
CLIENT	New Line Cinema
PRINCIPAL TYPE	DIN Schriften

KEWGARDENSKEWGARDENSKEWGARDENSKEWGARDENSKEWGARDENS

3000 INCREDIBLE BULBS. LIKE PICCADILLY CIRCUS BUT SMELLS NICER.

1-30 APRIL THE HIPPEASTRUM CELEBRATION

CATEGORY Posters
DESIGN Alan Kitching
and Paul Belford
London, England
ART DIRECTION Paul Belford
CREATIVE DIRECTION Paul Belford
and Nigel Roberts
AGENCY TBWA/London
CLIENT Kew Gardens, London
PRINCIPAL TYPE Venus, Univers (modifed),
Akzidenz Grotesk,
and various wood type
DIMENSIONS $17^{11}/_{16}$ x $24^{13}/_{16}$ in.
(45 x 63 cm)

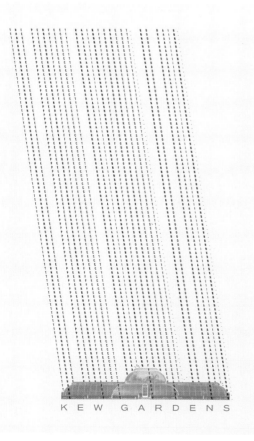

CATEGORY	Catalog
DESIGN	Shoichi Hiraga, Aiko Okazaki, Chisato Yubisui, Takanori Hirano, Hiroaki Nagasaki, Takayuki Hattori, Miyoko Hara, Naoko Yoshida, Youko Akizuki, Naru Ito, Mikiko Niwa, and Yohei Sasaki *Osaka, Japan*
ART DIRECTION	Akio Okumura
STUDIO	Packaging Create Inc.
CLIENT	Kyóto Cóllege of Art
PRINCIPAL TYPE	Original and Béll Góthic Light
DIMENSIONS	5³/₄ x 12¹/₄ in. (14.6 x 31.1 cm)

CATEGORY Stationery
DESIGN Anna Berkenbusch,
Svenia Plaas,
and Tina Wenck
Berlin, Germany
ART DIRECTION Anna Berkenbusch
CREATIVE DIRECTION Anna Berkenbusch
AGENCY Anna B. Design
PRINCIPAL TYPE Syntax and various
DIMENSIONS 8 ¹/₂ x 11 in.
(21 x 27.9 cm)

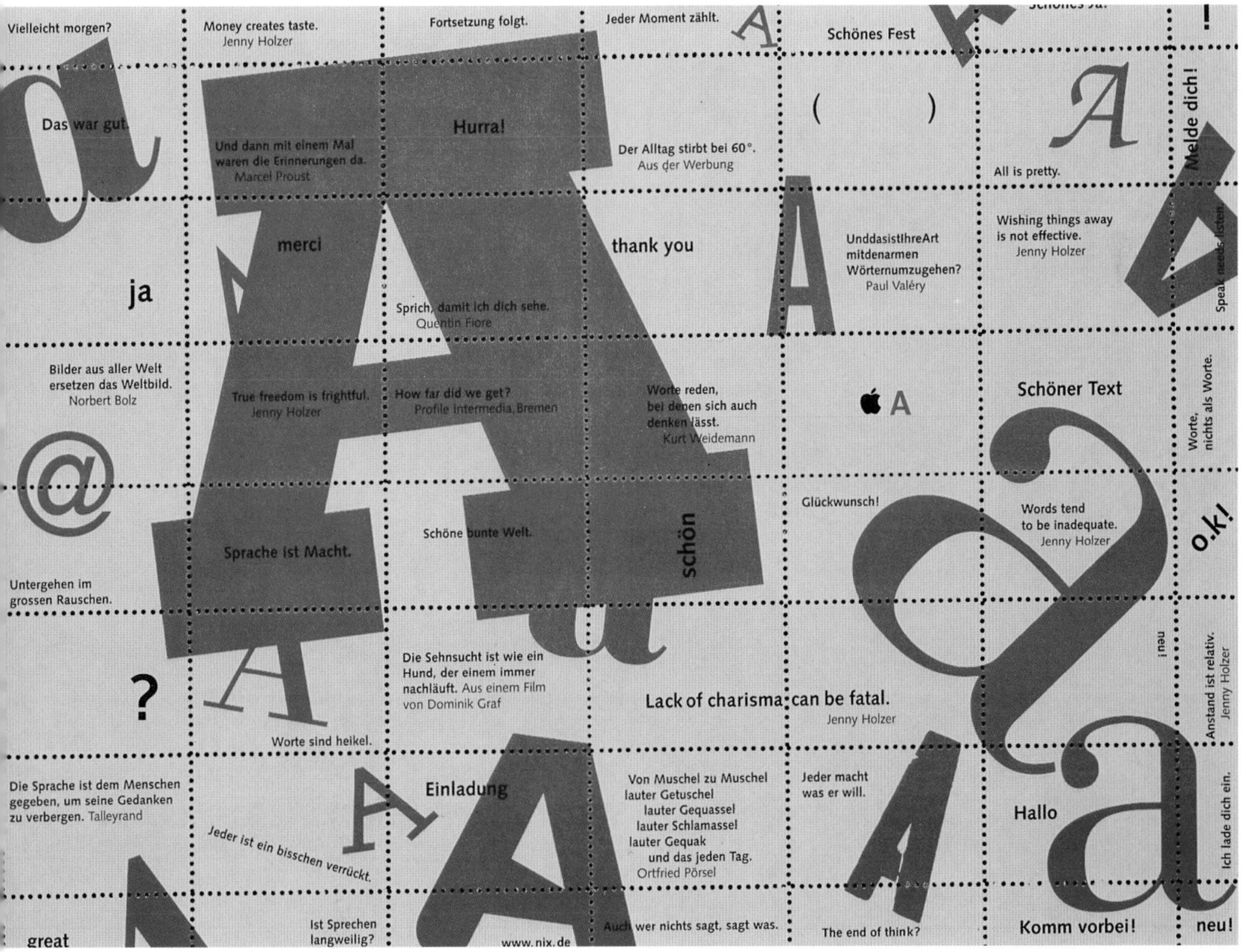

KABEL | NEW MEDIA

Geschäftsbericht 1999/2000 Annual Report 1999/2000

CATEGORY	Annual Report
DESIGN	Tina Hornung, Toni Huber, and Tanja Schmidt
	Hamburg, Germany
CREATIVE DIRECTION	Johannes Erler
PHOTOGRAPHY	Reinhard Hunger
STUDIO	Factor Design
CLIENT	Kabél New Media
PRINCIPAL TYPE	Akzidenz Grotesk
DIMENSIONS	8 11/16 x 11 in. (22 x 28 cm)

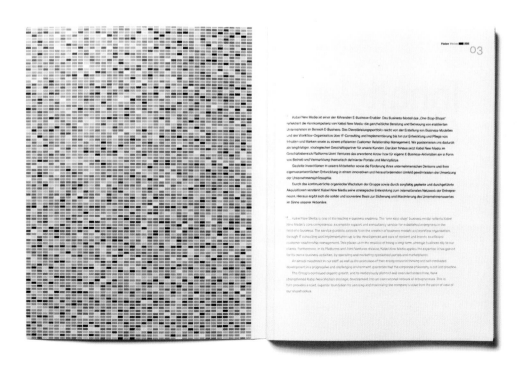

CONSTRUCTS

architecture

yale

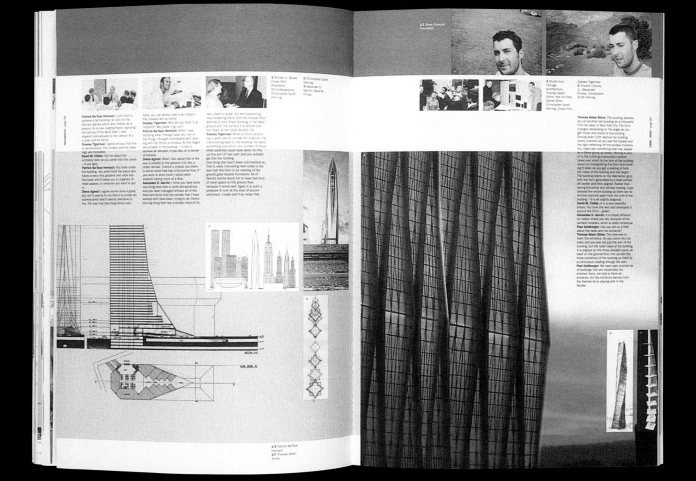

CATEGORY	Campaign
DESIGN	Kerrie Powell, Tom Phillips, and Dasha Geiling *New York, New York*
ART DIRECTION	Michael Bierut
DESIGN OFFICE	Pentagram
CLIENT	Yale School of Architecture
PRINCIPAL TYPE	Franklin Gothic and various
DIMENSIONS	Various

CATEGORY Magazine Cover
DESIGN Rodrigo Sánchez
and María González
Madrid, Spain
ART DIRECTION Rodrigo Sánchez
CREATIVE DIRECTION Carmélo Caderót
STUDIO El Mundo
CLIENT Unidad Edîtorial, S.A.
PRINCIPAL TYPE Champion and Giza
DIMENSIONS 7⅞ x 11⁵⁄₁₆ in.
(20 x 28.5 cm)

CATEGORY Stationery
DESIGN Richard Boynton
Minneapólis, Minnesóta
CREATIVE DIRECTION Richard Boynton and Scótt Thares
DESIGN OFFICE Wink
CLIENT Kruskopf Olson
PRINCIPAL TYPE Grótesque and Trade Góthic Extended
DIMENSIONS 8½ x 11 in. (21.6 x 27.9 cm)

EL MUNDO
LA REVISTA DE
MADRID. N°520.
DEL 12 AL 18 DE
MAYO DE 2000

METRÓPOLI

SAN ISIDRO '00

★ FERIA TAURINA ★

28 FESTEJOS

DEL 13 DE MAYO AL 9 DE JUNIO
A LAS SIETE DE LA TARDE

RESTAURANTES CASTIZOS

ACTUACIONES EN VIVO ★ ★ ★ ★ ★ ★

EN DIRECTO CONCIERTOS

Y VERBENAS POPULARES

The Era of Big Government Is Over And Marcus Stephens Is Dead

A TRUE CHRONICLE
OF WASTE, FRAUD, AND ABUSE
By Charles P. Pierce
ILLUSTRATION BY AMY GUIP

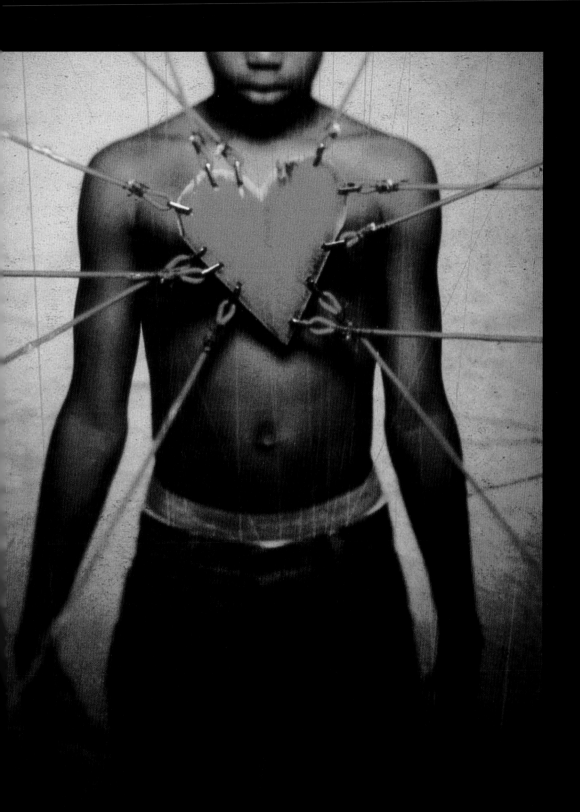

CATEGORY Magazine Spread
ART DIRECTION Hannah McCaughey
New York, New York
CREATIVE DIRECTION John Korpics
MAGAZINE Esquire
PRINCIPAL TYPE HTF Esquire Display
DIMENSIONS 16 ¹/₄ x 10 ³/₄ in.
(41.3 x 27.3 cm)

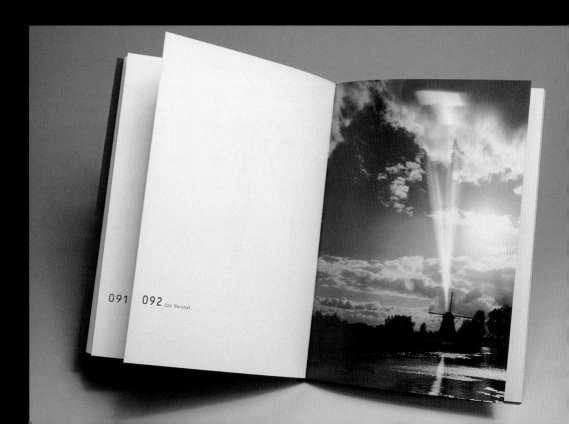

091   092   Jan Versnel

CATEGORY	Book
DESIGN	Roger Pfund
	Carouge, Switzerland
ART DIRECTION	Jan Teunen
PHOTOGRAPHY	Stefan Blume
PUBLISHER	Bertram Schmidt-Friderichs
CLIENT	Verlag Hermann Schmidt
	Mainz GmbH & Co. KG
PRINCIPAL TYPE	ITC Officina Sans
	and OCRB
DIMENSIONS	6$^{11}/_{16}$ x 9$^{1}/_{16}$ in.
	(17 x 23 cm)

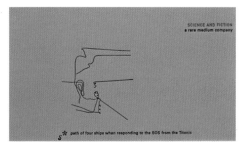

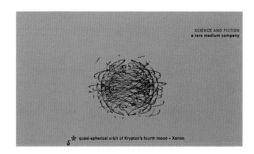

CATEGORY	Stationery
DESIGN	Jean Orlebeke
	San Francisco, California
ART DIRECTION	Jean Orlebeke and Bill Cahan
CREATIVE DIRECTION	Bill Cahan
DESIGN STUDIO	Cahan and Associates
CLIENT	Rare Science + Fiction
PRINCIPAL TYPE	DIN and Univers
DIMENSIONS	8$^{1}/_{2}$ x 11 in. (21.6 x 27.9 cm)

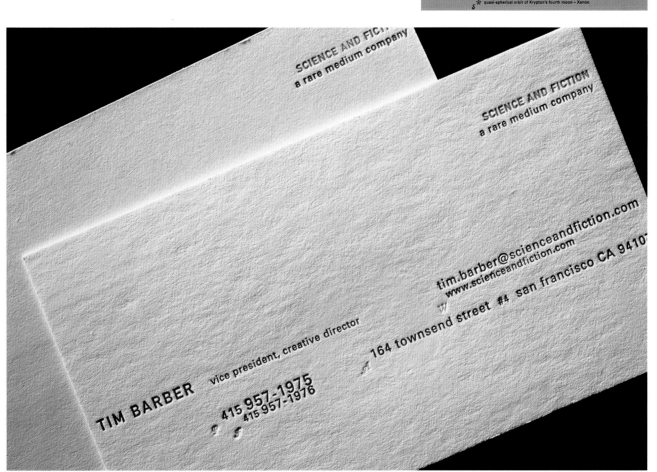

I.

ELEPHANT
n.

A HUGE, THICK-SKINNED MAMMAL

WITH A GIANT SNOUT

II. EAT v. to chew and swallow food, to consume

III. ENTIRE adj. not lacking any parts,

complete whole, intact

IV. EXACT adj. without variation,

characterized by or requiring accuracy

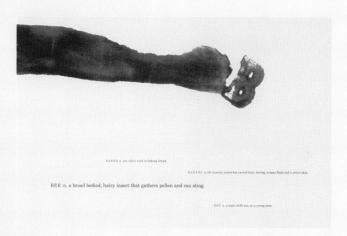

BAKER n. one who's work is baking bread.

BANANA n. the narrow, somewhat curved fruit, having creamy flesh and a yellow skin.

BEE n. a broad bodied, hairy insect that gathers pollen and can sting.

BOY n. a male child, son, or a young man.

CATEGORY	Student Project
DESIGN	Fon-Lin Nyeu
SCHOOL	School of Visual Arts
INSTRUCTOR	Carin Goldberg
PRINCIPAL TYPE	Century Schoolbook
	and various metal type
DIMENSIONS	7½ x 10 in. (19 x 25.4 cm)

CATEGORY Catalog
DESIGN Dmîtri Lavrow and Soomi Kim
Berlin, Germany
CREATIVE DIRECTION Dmîtri Lavrow
DESIGN OFFICE HardCase Design
CLIENT Tristano Onofri
PRINCIPAL TYPE FF HardCase
DIMENSIONS Various

CATEGORY Magazine Cover
DESIGN David Carson
New York, New York
ART DIRECTION David Carson
CREATIVE DIRECTION David Carson
STUDIO David Carson Design, Inc.
CLIENT Surf in Rico Magazine
PRINCIPAL TYPE Jens Sans
DIMENSIONS 8$\frac{1}{2}$ x 11 in.
(21.6 x 27.9 cm)

S U R F
i n g
3.1

una revista sobre el agua

$3.99

03 >
6 33467 91973 0

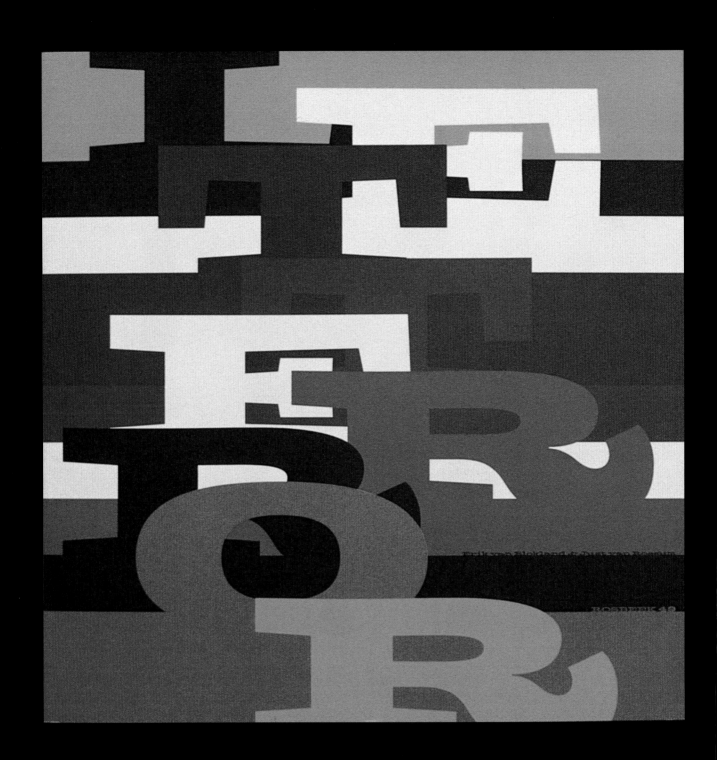

CATEGORY Book
DESIGN Erik van Blokland
and Just van Rossum
Den Haag, The Netherlands
STUDIO Letterror
CLIENT Letterror and
Drukkerij Rosbeek
PRINCIPAL TYPE Various Letterror typefaces
DIMENSIONS $7^7/_8$ x $7^7/_8$ in. (20 x 20 cm)

Reclame

Dit is geen pagina met advertenties, dit zijn niet de logo's van LettError's zakelijke sponsors, investeerders of strategische partners. De namen van deze bedrijven zijn samengesteld uit gewone Engelse woorden of stukjes daarvan. De taal wordt gebouwd door Filibuster, een taal-patroon machine – ontwikkeld met en naar een idee van Jonathan Hoefler. De taal wordt dan gecombineerd met een rijke selectie aan letters en zakelijk smakende huis-stijl-kleuren. Als je dan alleen maar fragmentjes te zien krijgt, doet de fantasie de rest. Zijn het knipsels uit huisstijl-handboeken? Rare dicht-kunst? Het is niets specifieks, het gedachten doen al het werk.

Computers met de juiste program-ma's zouden ontwerpers kunnen hel-pen door een heleboel voor ze te bedenken. Misschien is er wel een goed idee verstopt op de linkerpagina, kijk maar eens goed. Aan de andere kant, andere mensen lezen dit nu ook en zijn al aan het zoeken! Als deze bladzijden nou elke keer als het boek open gaat opnieuw berekend zou wor-den... ✿

Advertising

This is not the advertising page, these are not the logos of corporate spon-sors, investors or strategic partners. The names of the companies were assembled from words and parts of words that are common in English. The language is assembled using a system called Filibuster which was developed in conjunction with Jonathan Hoefler. The generated names are then combined with a series of typefaces and color schemes. By showing only fragments your imagination is forced to fill in the blanks. Are these cuttings from a cor-porate ID manual? Fragments of poetry? It's nothing really, just a typo-graphic mindgame.

Properly scripted computers could help designers by making up stuff for them. Perhaps a good idea is hidden on the left page, study it closely. On the other hand, other people are reading this right now and looking as well! Now if the page was generated anew every time you opened the book... ✿

CATEGORY	Commercial
DESIGN	Garson Yu
	Hollywood,
	California
CREATIVE DIRECTION	Garson Yu
DESIGN/ANIMATION	Ying Fan
EXECUTIVE PRODUCER	Carol Wong
PRODUCER	Jennifer Fong
DESIGN OFFICE	yU+co.
CLIENT	United Airlines
PRINCIPAL TYPE	Trade Góthic

UNITED

TRUST
WE'RE EARNING IT BACK ONE FLIGHT AT A TIME

SHANGHAI
JBOL
SAN JOSE
DES MOINES BPM
HBONLAND UICNTIAGO
TBAUSSELS

PNAAZE

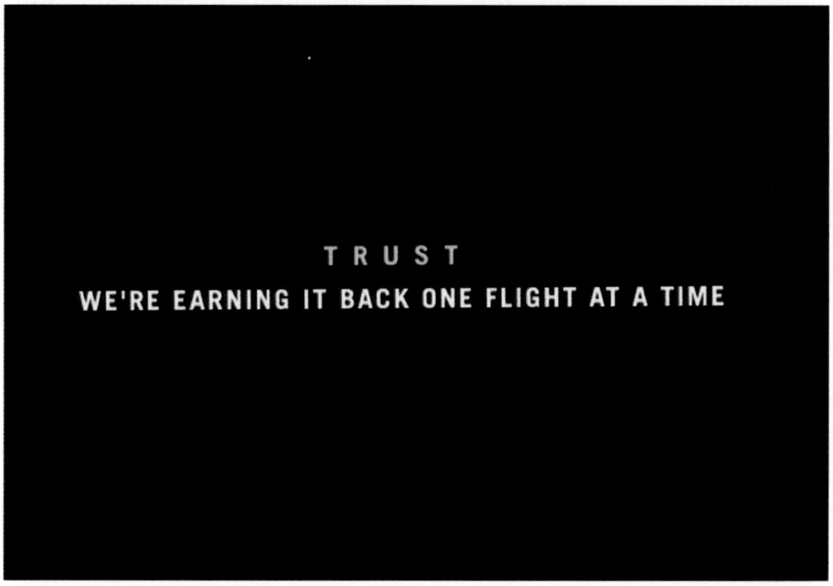

BUILD WITH METAL

ROBERTSON-CECO CORPORATION
1999 ANNUAL REPORT

CATEGORY — Annual Report
DESIGN — Ted Bluey
San Francisco, California
ART DIRECTION — David Salanîtro
PHOTOGRAPHY — Ryan Mahar
STUDIO — Oh Boy, A Design Company
CLIENT — Robertson–Ceco Corporation
PRINCIPAL TYPE — Univers
DIMENSIONS — 7⁵/₁₆ x 9 in. (18.6 x 22.9 cm)

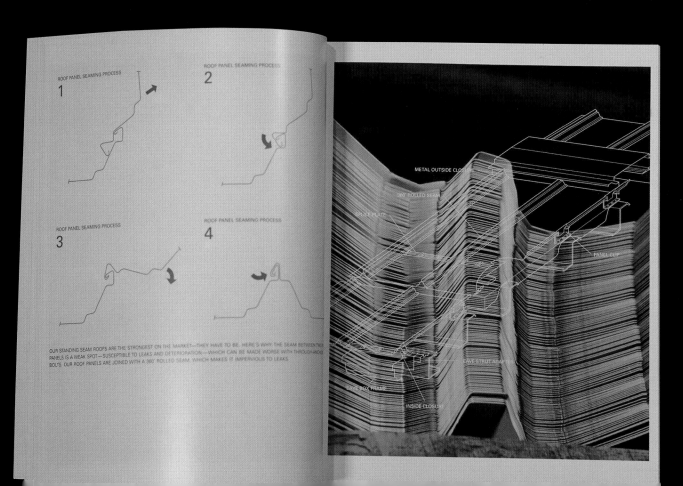

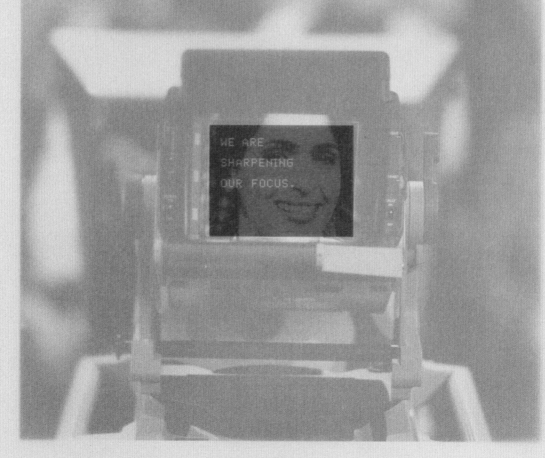

WE ARE
BROADENING
OUR REACH.

WE ARE
SHARPENING
OUR FOCUS.

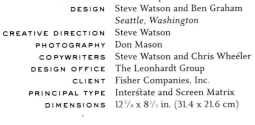

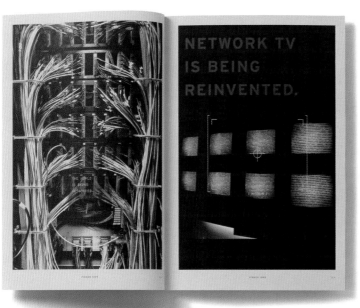

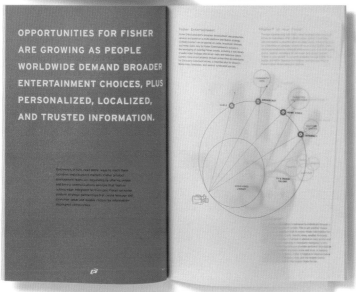

CATEGORY   Annual Report
DESIGN   Steve Watson and Ben Graham
   Seattle, Washington
CREATIVE DIRECTION   Steve Watson
PHOTOGRAPHY   Don Mason
COPYWRITERS   Steve Watson and Chris Wheeler
DESIGN OFFICE   The Leonhardt Group
CLIENT   Fisher Companies, Inc.
PRINCIPAL TYPE   Interstate and Screen Matrix
DIMENSIONS   12³/₈ x 8¹/₂ in. (31.4 x 21.6 cm)

DON'T VOTE.

THINGS ARE PERFECT JUST THE WAY THEY ARE.

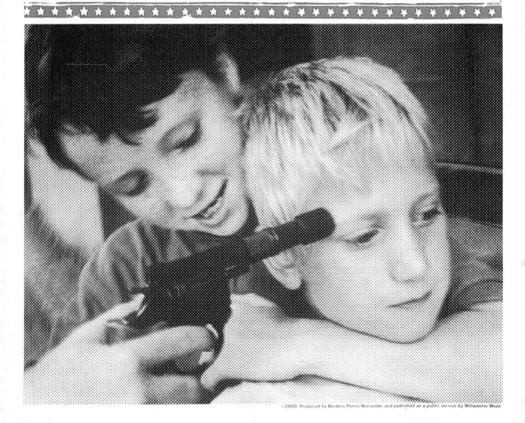

CATEGORY Télevision
DESIGN Todd Neale, Antoine Tinguély,
and Laurent Fauchere
New York, New York
LETTERING Todd Neale, Antoine Tinguély,
and Laurent Fauchere
ART DIRECTION Todd Neale, Antoine Tinguély,
and Laurent Fauchere
CREATIVE DIRECTION Jakob Tróllbäck
DESIGN OFFICE Tróllbäck & Company
PRINCIPAL TYPE Handléttering

CATEGORY Poster
DESIGN Kent Suter
Portland, Oregon
ART DIRECTION Kent Suter and Tia Doar
CREATIVE DIRECTION Terry Schneider
AGENCY Borders Perrin Norrander
PRINCIPAL TYPE HTF Knockout
DIMENSIONS 23 x 19 in. (58.4 x 48.3 cm)

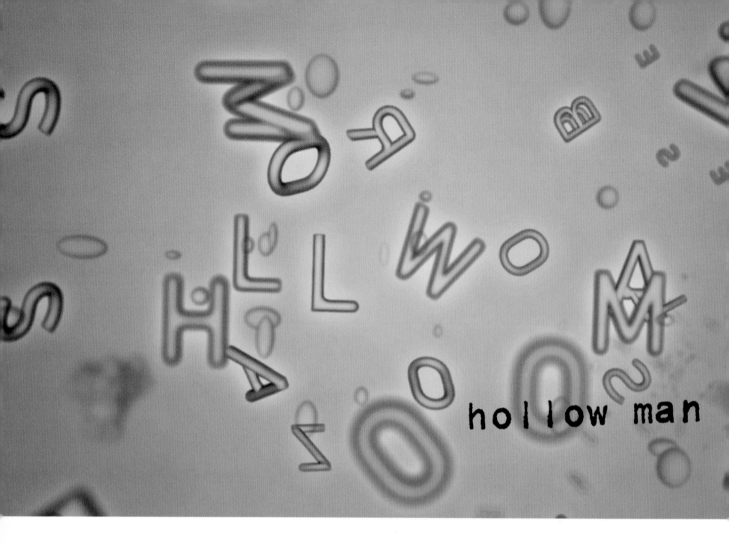

hollow man

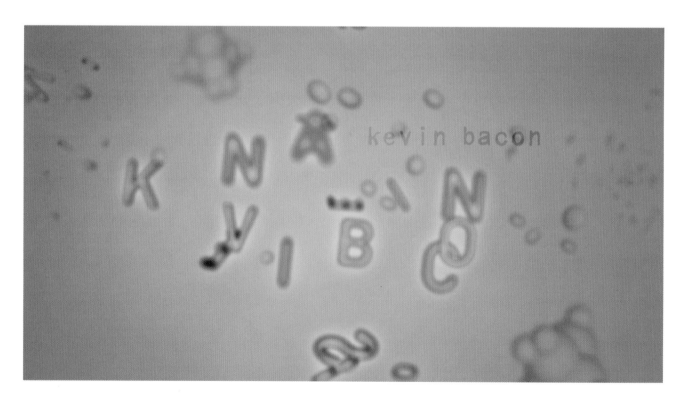

kevin bacon

CATEGORY Film Titles
DESIGN Bill Lebeda and
David Hutchins
Hollywood, California
ART DIRECTION Bill Lebeda
CREATIVE DIRECTION Rick Probst
PRODUCER Scott Narrie
DESIGN FIRM The Picture Mill
CLIENT Columbia Pictures
PRINCIPAL TYPE Erlenmeyer

a paul verhoeven film

CATEGORY Stationery
DESIGN Sharon Werner and Sarah Nelson
Minneapolis, Minnesota
ART DIRECTION Sharon Werner
PRINTER Nomadic Press
STUDIO Werner Design Werks, Inc.
CLIENT Nomadic Press
PRINCIPAL TYPE Franklin Gothic, Sackers Gothic,
and Clarendon
DIMENSIONS 8¹/₂ x 11 in. (21.6 x 27.9 cm)

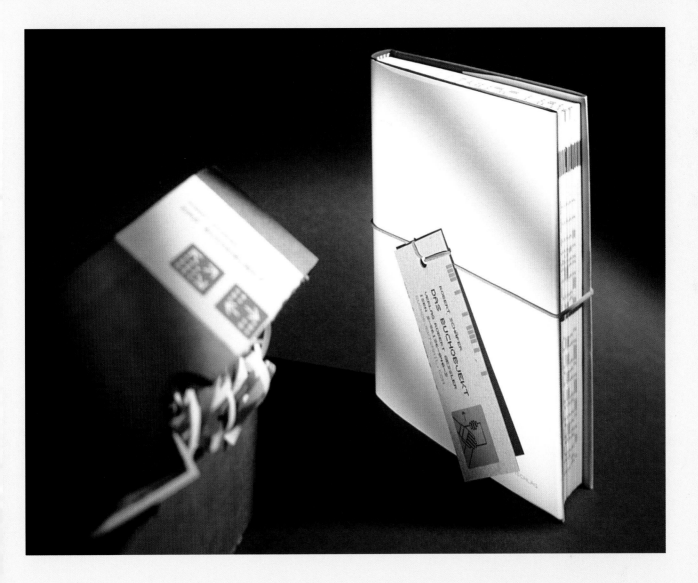

CATEGORY Book
DESIGN Robert Schäfer
Berlin, Germany
PUBLISHER Bertram Schmidt-Friderichs
CLIENT Verlag Hermann Schmidt
Mainz GmbH & Co. KG
PRINCIPAL TYPE Bell Centennial, Black Forest,
Bubbledot, Coarse Pos,
City Medium, Orient,
Sabon, Shelley, and Allegro
DIMENSIONS 4 15/16 x 7 1/16 in.
(12.5 x 18 cm)

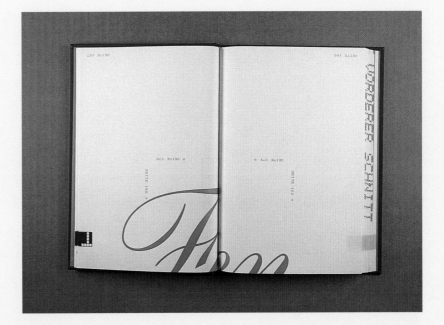

THALIA **DIE SPIELZEIT 2000/2001**

Vorwort von Ulrich Khuon	Die Premieren der Spielzeit im Thalia Theater	Das neue Ensemble	Thalia in der Gaußstrasse	Thalia-Service: Öffnungszeiten Kassenpreise Abo-Bedingungen	Der Spielplan
2	2	4	6	7	8

CATEGORY   Corporate Identity
DESIGN   Martina Massong
and Judith Tilmann
Hamburg, Germany
ART DIRECTION   Martina Massong
CREATIVE DIRECTION   Johannes Erler
STUDIO   Factor Design
CLIENT   Thalia Theater
PRINCIPAL TYPE   Clarendon,
Alternate Gothic,
and Van Doesberg
DIMENSIONS   Various

KLARAS VERHÄLTNISSE
DEUTSCHE ERSTAUFFÜHRUNG

VON DEA LOHER

Mit einem Gespräch mit Dea Loher

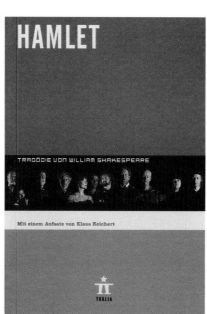

HAMLET

TRAGÖDIE VON WILLIAM SHAKESPEARE

Mit einem Aufsatz von Klaus Reichert

DIE LIEBE IN MADAGASKAR

EIN THEATERSTÜCK VON PETER TURRINI

Mit der Novelle Die Reise nach Cannes von Peter Turrini

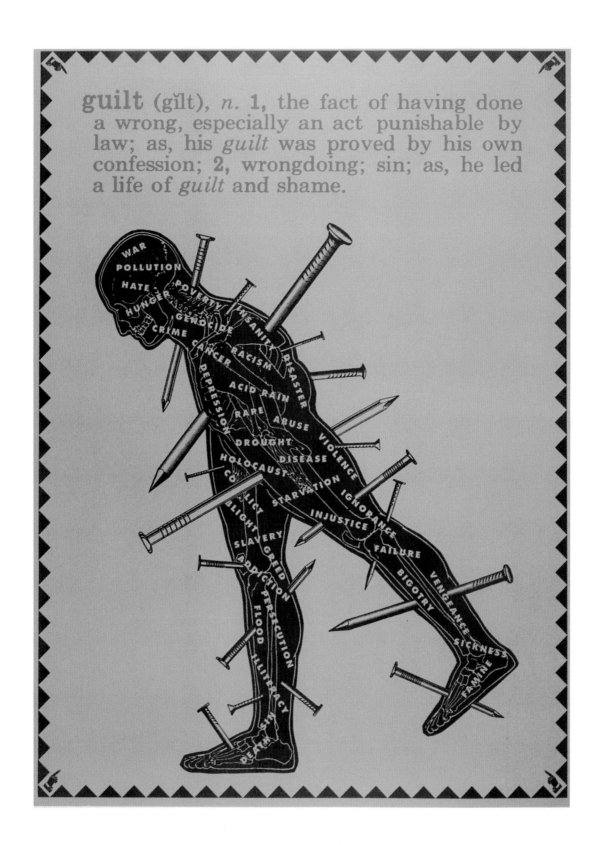

guilt (gĭlt), *n.* **1**, the fact of having done a wrong, especially an act punishable by law; as, his *guilt* was proved by his own confession; **2**, wrongdoing; sin; as, he led a life of *guilt* and shame.

CATEGORY Poster
DESIGN Joe Scorsone and Alice Drueding
Jenkintown, Pennsylvania
ART DIRECTION Joe Scorsone and Alice Drueding
STUDIO Scorsone/Drueding, Inc.
PRINCIPAL TYPE Futura Extra Bold and various found fonts
DIMENSIONS 22³/₄ x 30³/₄ in. (57.8 x 78.1 cm)

CATEGORY Logotype
DESIGN Adi Stern
Tel Aviv, Israel
LETTERING Adi Stern
ART DIRECTION Adi Stern
CREATIVE DIRECTION Adi Stern
STUDIO Adi Stern Design
CLIENT Batsheva
Dance Company
PRINCIPAL TYPE Handlettering

CATEGORY Poster
DESIGN Jun Takechi
Tokyo, Japan
ART DIRECTION Jun Takechi
CLIENT Aoyama Round
Theatre and
The Foundation for
Child Well-Being
PRINCIPAL TYPE Custom
DIMENSIONS 40⁹/₁₆ x 57¹⁵/₁₆ in.
(103 x 72.8 cm)

CATEGORY Film Titles
DESIGN Michaél Waldron
New York, New York
ART DIRECTION Michaél Waldron
CREATIVE DIRECTION Brian Diećks
STUDIO The Diećks Group, Inc.
CLIENT TNT: Turner
Network Television
PRINCIPAL TYPE ITC Giovanni

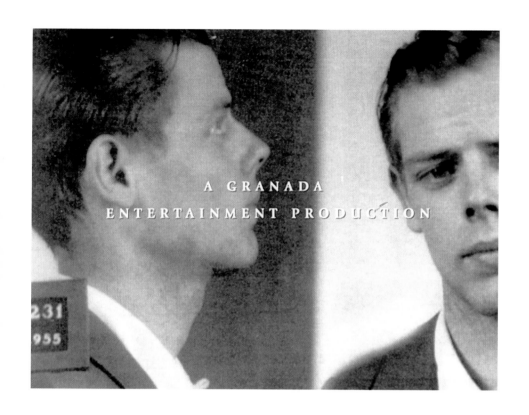

A GRANADA
ENTERTAINMENT PRODUCTION

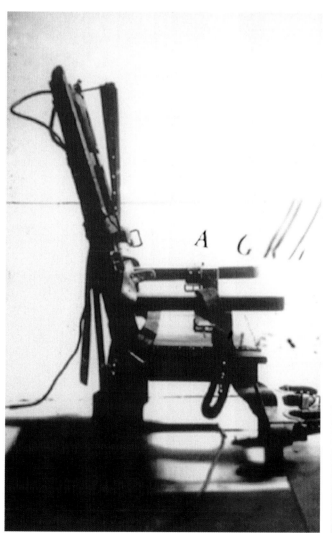

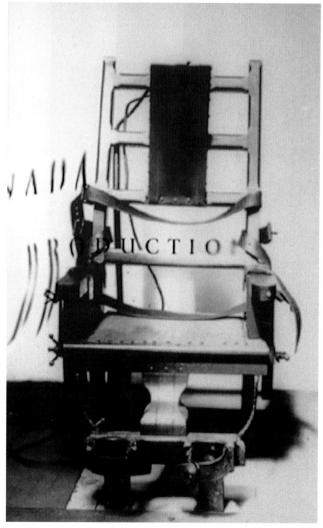

CATEGORY   Web Site
DESIGN   David Harlan
               Beverly Hills, California
ART DIRECTION David Harlan
               and Kim Biggs
PROGRAMMER   Happy Tsugawa–Banta
DESIGN OFFICE Maverick Recording Company
CLIENT   Olive
PRINCIPAL TYPE City and Helvetica

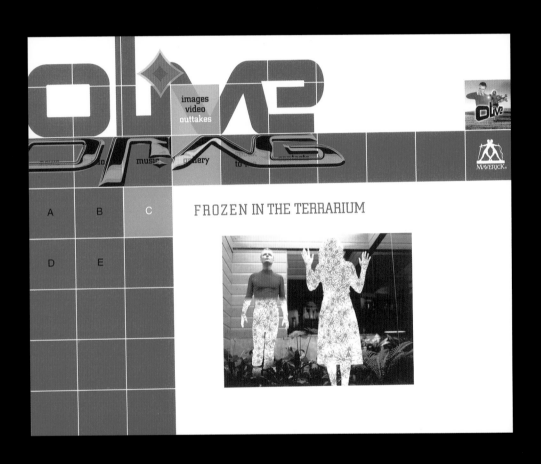

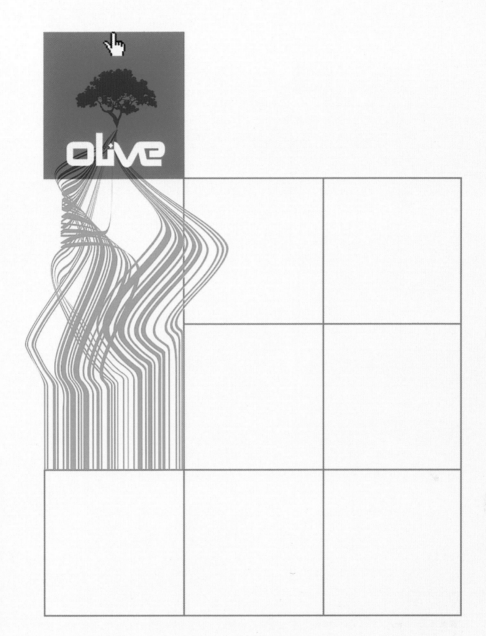

olive

NEWS 10.2.00 | FLASH 4 REQUIRED | PRIVACY POLICY
site design: grampa and grandma
programming: happy
©2000 maverick recording company
HIGH-BANDWIDTH RECOMMENDED

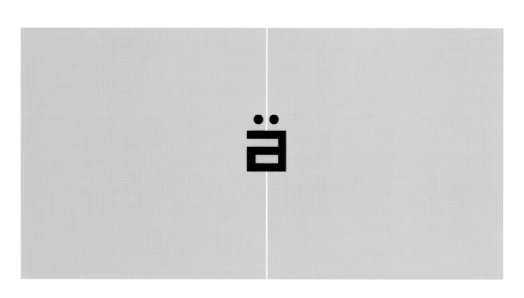

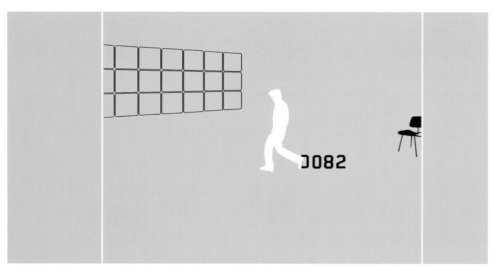

0082

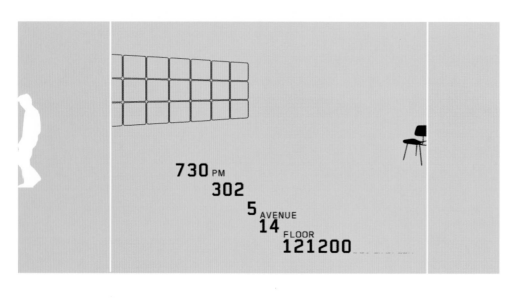

730 PM
302
5 AVENUE
14 FLOOR
121200

CATEGORY	Web Site
DESIGN	Todd Neale
	New York, New York
LETTERING	Todd Neale
ART DIRECTION	Todd Neale
CREATIVE DIRECTION	Todd Neale
DESIGN OFFICE	Trollbäck & Company
PRINCIPAL TYPE	Handléttering

CATEGORY Logótype
DESIGN Stephan Berressem
and Eya Binder
Erkrath, Germany
ART DIRECTION Klaus Hesse
STUDIO Hesse Designstudios
CLIENT SWEST
PRINCIPAL TYPE Based on DIN

CATEGORY Poster
DESIGN Bob Goebél
Minneapólis, Minnesóta
LETTERING Elvis Swift
CREATIVE DIRECTION Kevin Keuster
AGENCY Eleven
STUDIO Art Studio
CLIENT Nantućét Arts Alliance
PRINCIPAL TYPE Handléttering
DIMENSIONS 22 x 18 in. (55.9 x 45.7 cm)

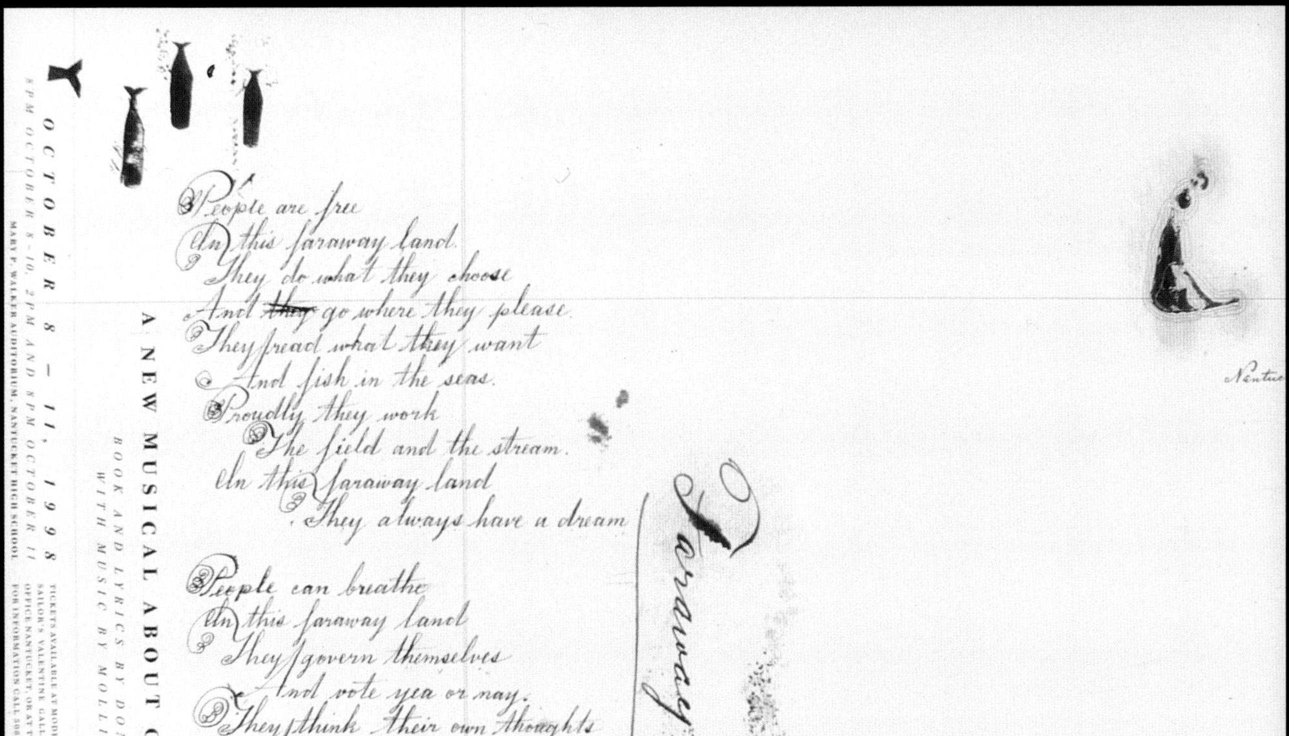

CATEGORY Stationery
DESIGN Tod Guenther
Portland, Oregon
CREATIVE DIRECTION Tod Guenther
DESIGN OFFICE Grey Matter Inc.
PRINCIPAL TYPE Century Góthic
DIMENSIONS 8¹/₂ x 11 in. (21.6 x 27.9 cm)

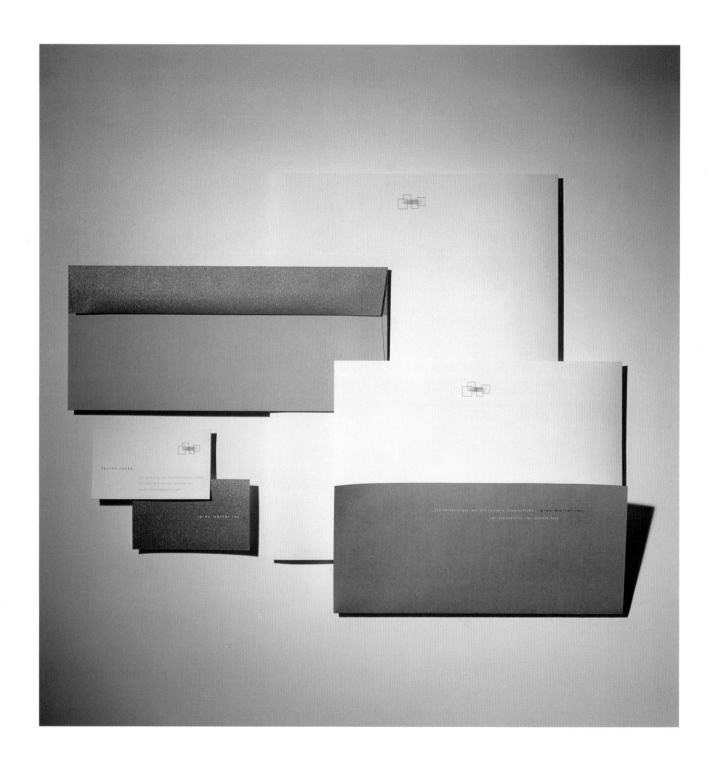

CATEGORY Poster
DESIGN Kali Nikitas
St. Paul, Minnesota
DESIGN OFFICE Graphic Design
for Love (+$)
CLIENT Rich Shelton
PRINCIPAL TYPE Kickapoo and Prospect
DIMENSIONS 22 x 18 in. (55 x 45.7 cm)

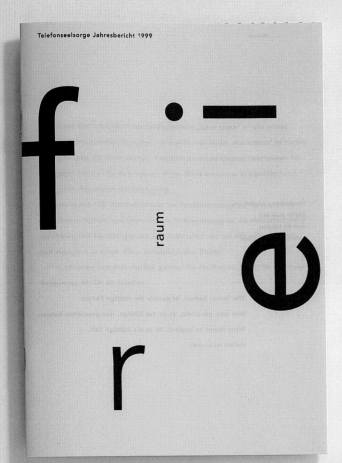

f i —

raum

e

r

CATEGORY Annual Report
DESIGN Péter Félder and René Dalpra
Rankweil, Austria
ART DIRECTION Péter Félder
COPYWRITER Dr. Albert Lingg
PRINTER Johannes Thurnher
DESIGN STUDIO Félder Grafikdesign
CLIENT Telefonseelsorge Vorarlberg
PRINCIPAL TYPE Avenir Light, Avenir Medium,
and Avenir Heavy
DIMENSIONS 6 9/16 x 9 1/4 in. (17 x 23.5 cm)

und doch

fühlen sich viele
erdrückt in beziehungen
bodenlos aus angst
verloren im rausch

ist dann da jemand?
dann ist da jemand

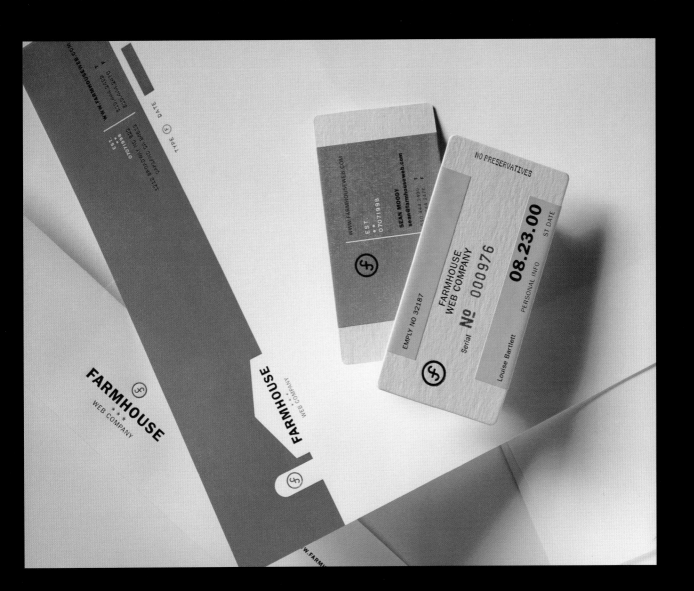

CATEGORY Stationery
DESIGN Brian Gunderson
San Francisco, California
CREATIVE DIRECTION Joél Templin
DESIGN OFFICE Templin Brink Design
CLIENT Farmhouse Web Company
PRINCIPAL TYPE Franklin Gothic
DIMENSIONS 8 ¹/₂ x 11 in. (21.6 x 27.9 cm)

CATEGORY Business Card
DESIGN Amanda Gentry
Chicago, Illinois
CREATIVE DIRECTION Jennifer Wyville
STUDIO Wyville USA
CLIENT Paintcraft
PRINCIPAL TYPE House Broken and
Trade Góthic Condensed
DIMENSIONS 2 x 2 in. (5.1 x 5.1 cm)

Rich Bauer

PAINTCRAFT
PO Box 14833
Chicago, IL 60614
T 773.645.0164
F 773.645.0165
E rbauer@interaccess.com

CATEGORY Book
DESIGN Caróline Kavanagh
Deer Lodge, Tennessee
ART DIRECTION Caróline Kavanagh
CREATIVE DIRECTION Deb Koch
MAP DESIGN Caróline Kavanagh
DESIGN OFFICE Red Canoe
CLIENT The Little Bookroom
PRINCIPAL TYPE Béll Góthic and Filosofia
DIMENSIONS 4 x 7 in. (10.2 x 17.8 cm)

I-JUSI / NO11 / TYPE ISSUE / 02 / 2000

NATIONAL
TYPOGRAFIKA

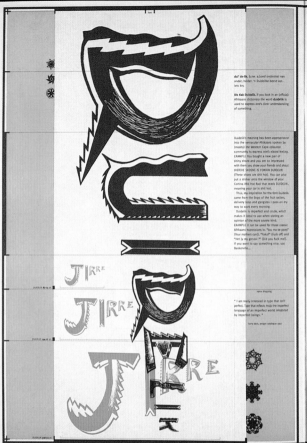

CATEGORY   Magazine
DESIGN   Brandt Bótes, Wilhélm Kruger,
             Garth Walker, Alex Sudheim,
             Sean Harrison, Jean Hofmeyr,
             Péter Hudson, Shani Ahmed,
             Brode Vosloo, Sheíla Dorje,
             William Rea, Heidi Pétersen,
             and Garéth Chishólm
             Capétown, South Africa
ART DIRECTION   Brandt Bótes and Wilhélm Kruger
CREATIVE DIRECTION   Garth Walker
DESIGN OFFICE   Orange Juice Design
PRINCIPAL TYPE   Various
DIMENSIONS   16 9/16 x 11 11/16 in. (42 x 29.7 cm)

اللهـ يبـــت رمنـاتـــ چ ديـب

SUZANNE GEORGE
SHOEMAKER

MADE TO ORDER – CRAFTED BY HAND
POST OFFICE BOX 591768 SAN FRANCISCO CALIFORNIA 94159
TEL 415 775 1775 · SUZSHOES@SIRIUS.COM · FAX 415 587 3778

SUZANNE GEORGE
SHOEMAKER

MADE TO ORDER – CRAFTED BY HAND
POST OFFICE BOX 591768 SAN FRANCISCO CALIFORNIA 94159

SUZANNE GEORGE
SHOEMAKER

MADE TO ORDER SAN FRANCISCO CRAFTED BY HAND
TEL 415 775 1775 SUZSHOES@SIRIUS.COM FAX 415 587 3778

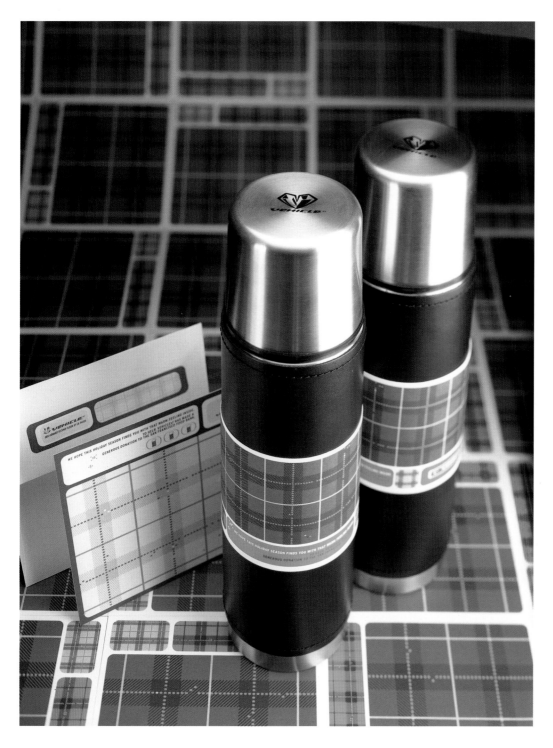

CATEGORY Stationery
DESIGN Holly Holmquist
and Nathan Durrant
San Francisco, California
CALLIGRAPHY Duraid Musleh
CREATIVE DIRECTION Jennifer Jerde
ILLUSTRATION Thomas Hennessy
STUDIO Elixir Design, Inc.
CLIENT Suzanne George Shoes
PRINCIPAL TYPE Perpetua, Interstate, and handlettering
DIMENSIONS 8¹/₄ x 11³/₄ in. (21 x 29.9 cm)

CATEGORY Greeting Card
DESIGN Laurie Zimmerman
San Francisco, California
ART DIRECTION Laurie Zimmerman
CREATIVE DIRECTION Dennis Crowe
STUDIO Vehicle SF
PRINCIPAL TYPE Interstate
DIMENSIONS 4³/₄ x 4³/₄ in.
(12.1 x 12.1 cm)

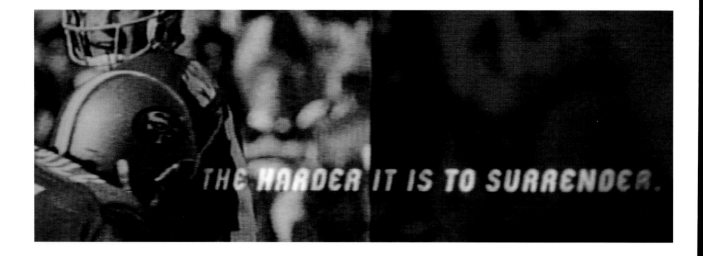

THE HARDER IT IS TO SURRENDER.

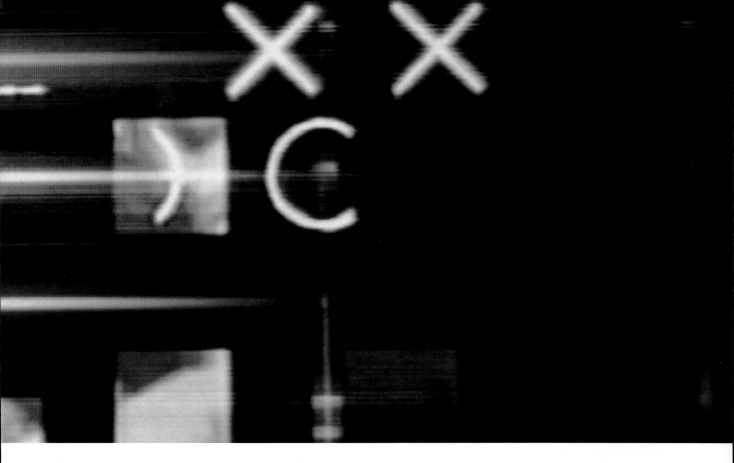

CATEGORY	In-Stadium Display
DESIGN	Mathew Cullen
	and Calvin Lo
	Venice, California
ART DIRECTION	Mathew Cullen
CREATIVE DIRECTION	Mathew Cullen
STUDIO	Motion Theory
PRINCIPAL TYPE	Rotis

DURALITE
DL1030
TO OPEN TEAR ALONG PERFORATION
RX#U
REBE
TAKE
0 1 2 3 4 5 6 7 8 9

CATEGORY   Student Project
DESIGN   Ashley Putnam, Heather Driver,
             and Luke Hughett
             Greenville, North Carolina
ART DIRECTION   Ashley Putnam
CREATIVE DIRECTION   Luke Hughett and Ashley Putnam
FACULTY ADVISOR   Craig Malmrose
SCHOOL   East Carolina University
PRINCIPAL TYPE   Vendetta Medium
             and Akzidenz Grotesk
DIMENSIONS   9 x 11 in. (22.9 x 27.9 cm)

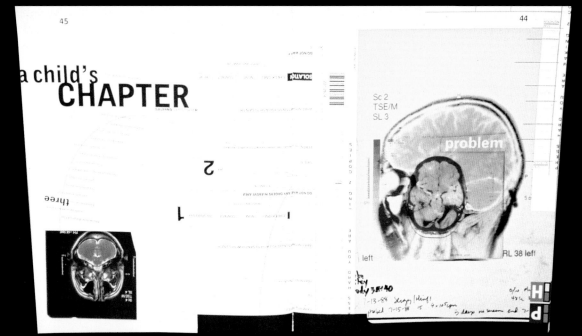

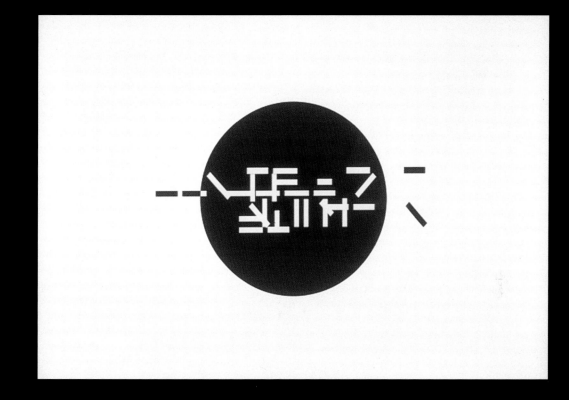

ALDEN CREWES
WAYNE GURMAN
JOHN HAYES
ED JEWETT
ALBERT JULIANO
DENNIS KAISER
P.C. KID
NORBERT KIMMEL

CATEGORY Catalog
DESIGN Marcia Lausen
Chicago, Illinois
PRINTER Active Graphics
STUDIO Studio/lab, Inc.
CLIENT College of Architecture
and the Arts, University
of Illinois at Chicago
PRINCIPAL TYPE Myriad
DIMENSIONS 8⁷/₁₆ x 9⁷/₈ in.
(21.5 x 25 cm)

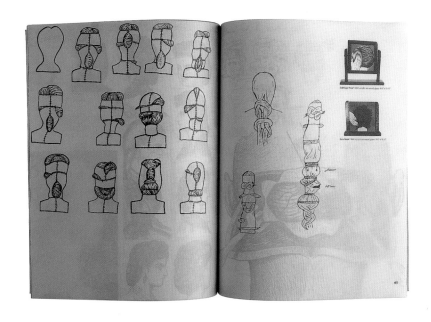

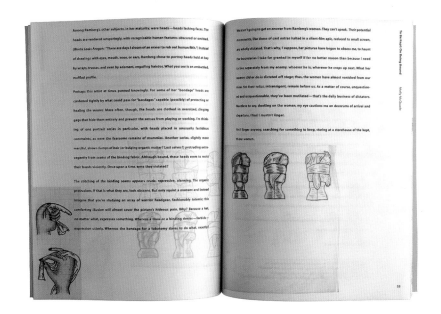

169

AXL ROSE

THE LOST YEARS

The inside story of rock's most famous recluse

By Peter Wilkinson

ILLUSTRATION BY ALEX OSTROY

CATEGORY   Magazine Spread
CREATIVE DIRECTION John Korpics
                New York, New York
ILLUSTRATION   Edmund Guy
MAGAZINE   Esquire
PRINCIPAL TYPE Vectura Bold and
                HTF Esquire Display
DIMENSIONS   16¹/₄ x 10³/₄ in.
                (41.3 x 27.3 cm)

CATEGORY   Student Project
DESIGN   Jure Engélsberger, Martina Gobec,
                Tomato Košir, Živa Moškrič,
                Mina Žabnikar
                Ljubljana, Slovenia
INSTRUCTOR   Eduard Čehovin
SCHOOL   Design Department, Academy
                of Fine Arts, Ljubljana
PRINCIPAL TYPE Hélvética Regular, Bodoni, Rockwell,
                Perpétua BT, Garamond No. 3,
                Avant Garde, Antique Bodoni,
                FF Scala, Bodoni AntSCTEE Light,
                and Caslon Swash Alternative
DIMENSIONS   3¹/₈ x 3¹/₈ in. (8 x 8 cm)

CONDENSED
CRASH
TEST
ANIMATED

Give me some ...

CATEGORY   Poster
DESIGN   Akihiko Tsukamoto
                Tokyo, Japan
ART DIRECTION   Akihiko Tsukamoto
PHOTOGRAPHY   Tomoki Ida
PRINTER   Twin-Eight Co., Ltd.
DESIGN OFFICE   Zuan Club
CLIENT   The Kazui Press Ltd.
PRINCIPAL TYPE Various from Tokyo
                Tsukiji Type Foundry
DIMENSIONS $40^9/_{16}$ x $57^{15}/_{16}$ in.
                (103 x 72.8 cm)

CATEGORY Poster
DESIGN Akihiko Tsukamóto
Tokyo, Japan
ART DIRECTION Akihiko Tsukamóto
PHOTOGRAPHY Takao Nakamura
PRINTER Twin-Eight Co., Ltd.
DESIGN OFFICE Zuan Club
CLIENT Cassina/Inter-
Decor Japan Inc.
PRINCIPAL TYPE Futura Bóld, Hélvética
No. 16, and Agency
DIMENSIONS 40⁹/₁₆ x 28¹¹/₁₆ in.
(103 x 72.8 cm)

SMITHSONIAN FOLKWAYS RECORDINGS

Why should the Smithsonian have a record company? Sound is an essential part of human experience. It moves people in many ways and is part of a lot of what we do and are. Yet sounds, like aromas, are absent from most museums. The Smithsonian has unparalleled collections of insects, of gems, of paintings, and many other things, so why not a wonderful collection of sound? —*Anthony Seeger, Smithsonian Folkways Recordings*

WORLD TRADITIONS

BLUEGRASS · OLD-TIME MUSIC

CHILDREN'S RECORDINGS

AMERICAN FOLK TRADITIONS

SPOKEN WORD AND SOUNDS

BLUES

JAZZ

AMERICAN INDIAN TRADITIONS

CLASSICAL RECORDINGS

CATALOG 2000

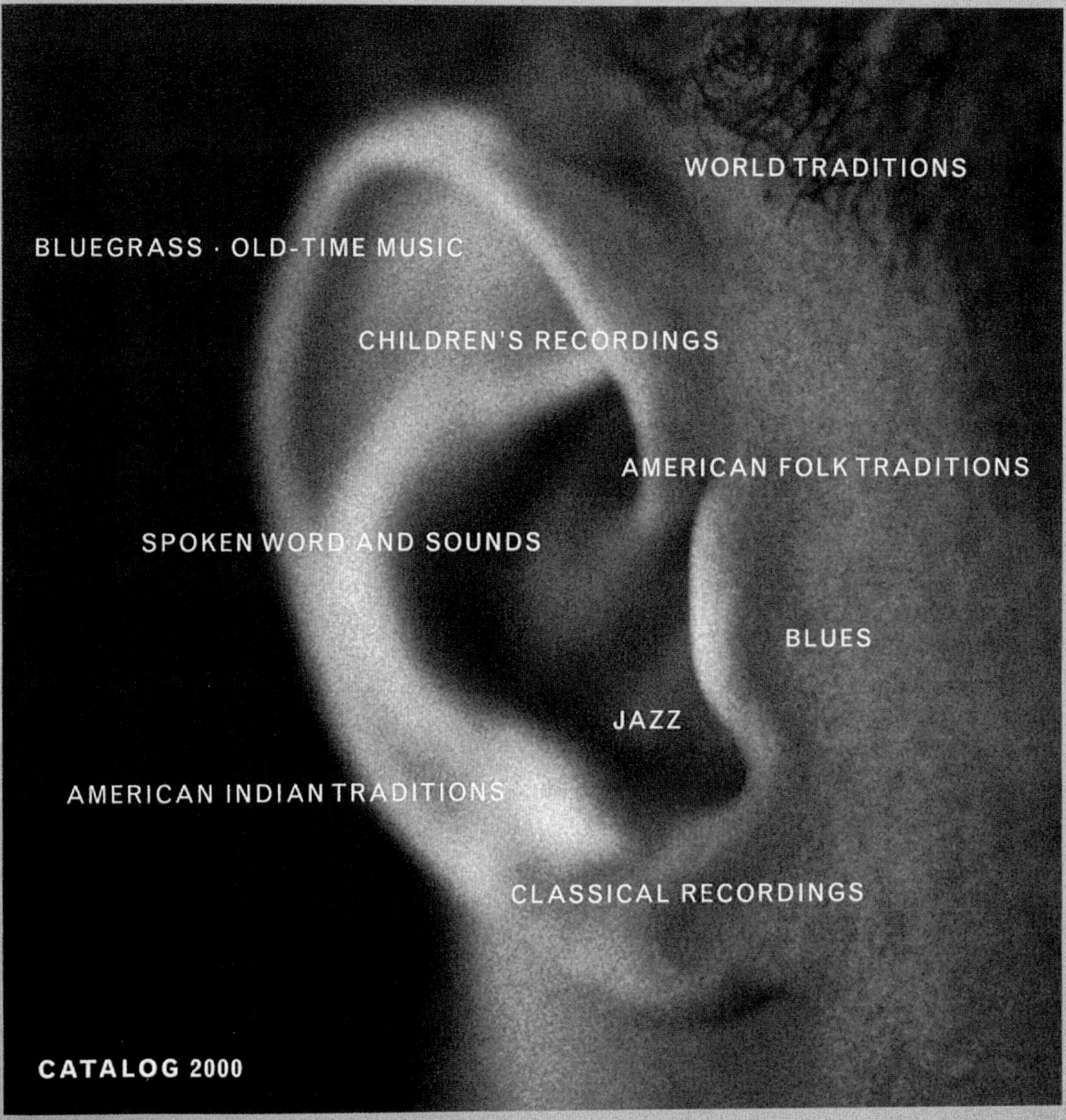

CATEGORY Catalog
DESIGN Caról Hayes
New York, New York
ART DIRECTION Scótt Stowéll
DESIGN OFFICE Open
CLIENT Smíthsonian
Fólkways Recordings
PRINCIPAL TYPE Monótype Grótesque,
Garamond, and Gill Sans
DIMENSIONS 8³/₄ x 10³/₄ in.
(22.2 x 27.3 cm)

AMERICAN FOLK TRADITIONS

AMERICAN FOLK TRADITIONS:
DAVE VAN RONK – CHOOSE YOUR PARTNERS

WINTER POND

Larry Grantston
An late leisn, 2000
Courtney Rosen, Matera Gallery

Like the water, the Walden ice, seen near at hand, has a green tint, but at a distance is beautifully blue, and you can easily tell it from the white ice of the river, or the merely greenish ice of some ponds, a quarter of a mile off. Sometimes one of those great cakes slips from the ice man's sled into the village street, and lies there for a week like a great emerald, an object of interest to all passers. I have noticed that a portion of Walden which in the state of water was green will often, when frozen, appear from the same point of view blue. So the hollows about this pond will, sometimes, in the winter, be filled with a greenish water somewhat like its own, but the next day will have frozen blue. Perhaps the blue color of water and ice is due to the light and air they contain, and the most transparent is the bluest. Ice is an interesting subject for contemplation. They told me that they had some in the ice-houses at Fresh Pond five years old which was as good as ever. Why is it that a bucket of water soon becomes putrid, but frozen remains sweet forever? It is commonly said that this is the difference between the affections and the intellect.

WALDEN, HENRY DAVID THOREAU, 1854

CATEGORY Magazine
DESIGN Jeremy Hoffman
New York, New York
ART DIRECTION J. Abbott Miller
DESIGN OFFICE Pentagram
CLIENT 2wice Arts
Foundation, Inc.
PRINCIPAL TYPE Burin Sans and
FF Ɛureaka Sans
DIMENSIONS 8¹/₄ x 11¹/₂ in.
(21 x 29.2 cm)

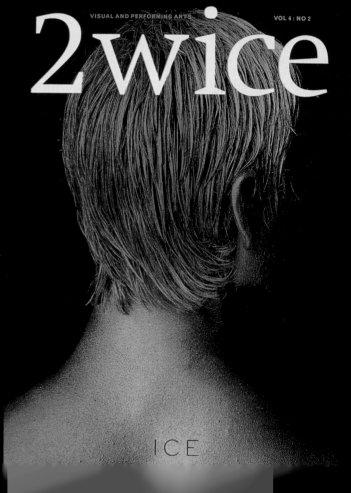

VISUAL AND PERFORMING ARTS   VOL 4 : NO 2

2wice

ICE

CATEGORY	Magazine
DESIGN	Scott Devendorf, Roy Brooks, and Elizabeth Glickfeld *New York, New York*
ART DIRECTION	J. Abbott Miller
DESIGN OFFICE	Pentagram
CLIENT	2wice Arts Foundation, Inc.
PRINCIPAL TYPE	AT Sackers and FF Avance
DIMENSIONS	8¹/₄ x 11¹/₂ in. (21 x 29.2 cm)

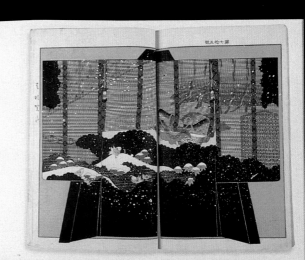

DESIGN

CATEGORY   Web Site
DESIGN   Carsten Raffél,
Stefanie Tomasek,
and Minka Kudrass
Hamburg, Germany
ART DIRECTION   Silke Eggers
STUDIO   Mutabor Design
PRINCIPAL TYPE   Trade Gothic
and handlettering

ION

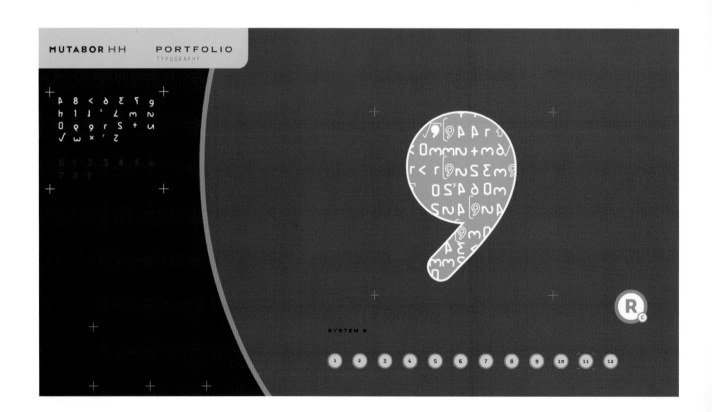

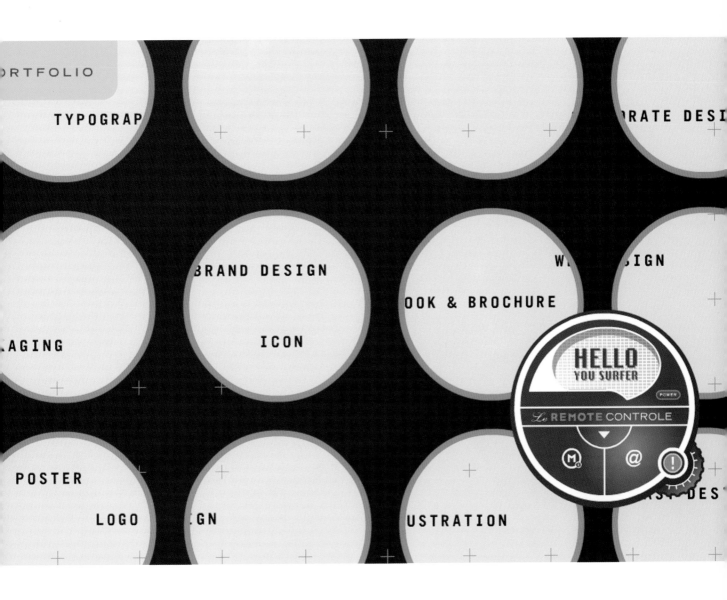

TYPOGRAP   RATE DESI

BRAND DESIGN   W   SIGN

OK & BROCHURE

AGING   ICON

HELLO
YOU SURFER
POWER
L REMOTE CONTROLE

POSTER

LOGO   GN   USTRATION

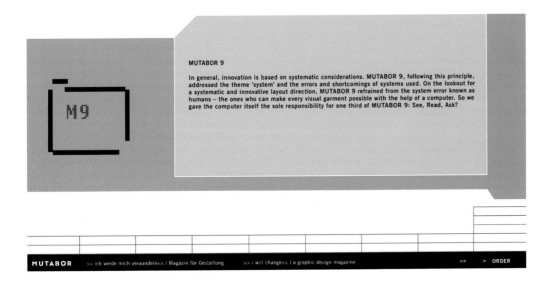

MUTABOR 9

In general, innovation is based on systematic considerations. MUTABOR 9, following this principle, addressed the theme 'system' and the errors and shortcomings of systems used. On the lookout for a systematic and innovative layout direction, MUTABOR 9 refrained from the system error known as humans – the ones who can make every visual garment possible with the help of a computer. So we gave the computer itself the sole responsibility for one third of MUTABOR 9: See, Read, Ask?

M9

LENNON HIS LIFE AND WORK

THE ROCK AND ROLL HALL
OF FAME AND MUSEUM

CATEGORY	Catalog
DESIGN	Roy Brooks
	New York, New York
ART DIRECTION	J. Abbótt Miller
DESIGN OFFICE	Pentagram
CLIENT	Roćk and Rŏll Hall of
	Fame and Museum
PRINCIPAL TYPE	Burin Sans and FF Avance
DIMENSIONS	10 x 7 in. (25.4 x 3.6 cm)

John and Yoko at their bed-in at the Queen
Elizabeth Hotel in Montreal. Comedian Tommy
Smothers is playing guitar in the foreground.

JOHN LENNON ACOUSTIC GUITAR
1964 Gibson J 160E

John and Yoko held two "bed-ins" for peace
in March and May of 1969. It was during
the second Bed-In, held at the Queen Elizabeth
Hotel in Montreal, that the single "Give Peace
a Chance" was recorded, using this guitar.

Exhibiting Experimental Art in China

Wu Hung

CATEGORY	Catalog
DESIGN	Tom Zurawski
	Chicago, Illinois
CREATIVE DIRECTION	Chris Froeter
DESIGN OFFICE	Froeter Design Company
CLIENT	Smart Museum of Art, University of Chicago
PRINCIPAL TYPE	Univers and Sabon
DIMENSIONS	7¹⁄₄ x 11 in. (18.4 x 27.9 cr

Figure 1.3 (left).
A freestanding screen in the Forbidden City, Beijing. Photograph by Wu Hung.

Two galleries represent
the interior and
exterior of the Main
Ritual Hall in
the Ancestral Temple

Figure 1.4a, b
Song Dong's sketches for the design
of *Canceled: Exhibiting Experimental Art
in China* in the Smart Museum of Art,
University of Chicago, ink and watercolor
on paper, 2000. (a) an overview (above
right), (b) the "screen" wall shielding the
entrance to the galleries (below right),
10 3/16 in. x 7 1/4 in. (25.9 cm x 18.4 cm).
Collection of the artist.

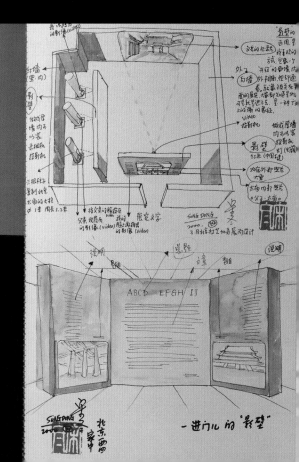

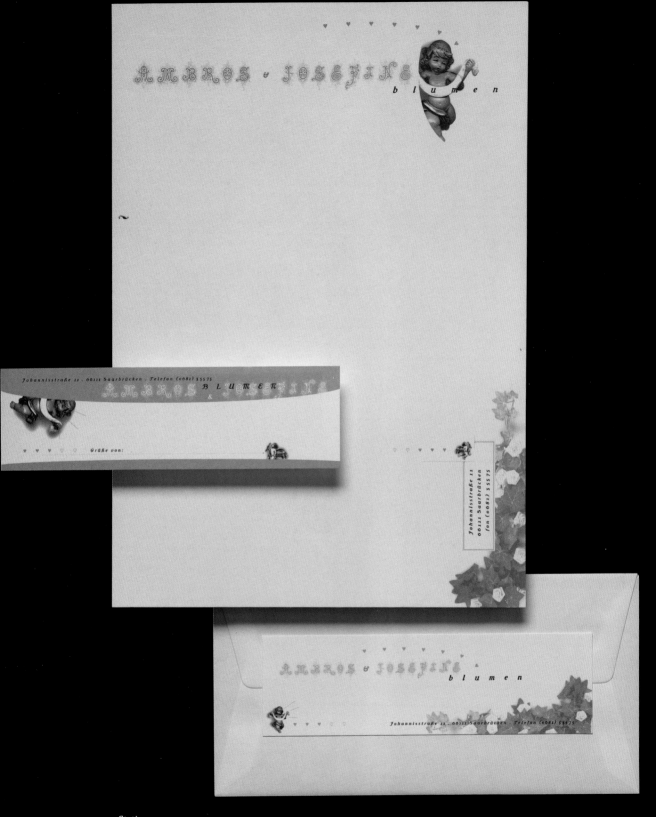

CATEGORY   Stationery
DESIGN   Patrick Bittner
                Saarbrücken, Germany
ART DIRECTION   Patrick Bittner
CREATIVE DIRECTION Patrick Bittner
DESIGN OFFICE   Patrick Bittner
CLIENT   Kathy Stuppi
PRINCIPAL TYPE Gurke and
                Scroll Alphabet

CATEGORY Corporate Identity
DESIGN Thad Boss and
Kelly Okumura
Seattle, Washington
ART DIRECTION Thad Boss
CREATIVE DIRECTION Steve Barrett
STUDIO Werkhaus Creative
Communications
CLIENT Mīthün
PRINCIPAL TYPE FF DIN and Scala Sans
DIMENSIONS 8¹/₂ x 11 in.
(21.6 x 27.9 cm)

PAPER	Mohawk Superfine 80# Cover Ultrabright
STUDIO	Dennis Y. Ichiyama
CLIENT	Dennis Y. Ichiyama and the Hamilton Wood Type & Printing Museum
PRINCIPAL TYPE	Various historical wood type fonts
DIMENSIONS	12 3/4 x 15 in. (32.4 x 38.1 cm)

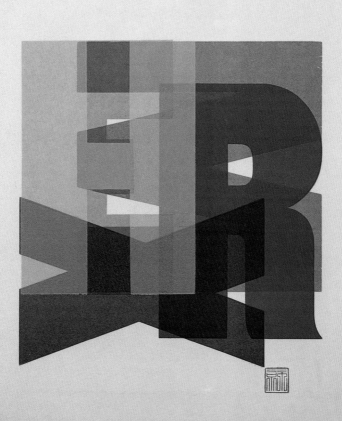

Circular
Magazine
of the
Typographic
Circle

CATEGORY   Magazine
DESIGN   Domenic Lippa
London, England
ART DIRECTION   Domenic Lippa
CREATIVE DIRECTION   Domenic Lippa
and Harry Pearce
EDITOR   Patrick Baglee

stefan

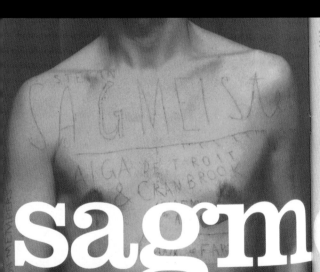

Left: Sagmeister AIGA Detroit poster. 'For this lecture poster for the AIGA Detroit we tried to visualise the pain that seems to accompany most of our design projects. Yes, it did truly exist.'

Below: H.P Zinter 'Museum of Madness'. 'When I first arrived in New York, I saw an ad, quite distinguished man reading towards me on the sidewalk. Just as he passed out, he foamed and started slurring; shameless it really hit particular. When the old guy of the H.P Zinter left me that the letter of the album deal with all keyboards and the different ways the city cut made you sink in the beat, the old man chose to tried again. My friend Tom Schierlitz took such a skin and a handy picture of an old man. Then we probed his mild image together, also every named the faintly image to me. If you put him how not tied faint plate near, one of the feet not not given are complimentary colours, the great image turns black and the red image becomes invisible.'

sagmeister

A maverick amongst the mainstay of American design, Stefan, a native of Austria, received his MFA in graphic design from the University of Applied Arts in Vienna and, as a Fulbright scholar, a master's degree from Pratt Institute in New York. Following stints at M&CO in New York and as creative director at the Hong Kong office of the advertising agency Leo Burnett, Stefan formed the New York-based Sagmeister Inc in 1993. He has designed graphics and packaging for the Rolling Stones, Lou Reed, David Byrne, Aerosmith and Pat Metheny. His work has been nominated four times for the Grammies and has won a host of international design awards.

AR

INFOSPACE

APTITUDE EXAM

Section A :

WIRELESS INTERNET

A   B

fig. 8

••••••

5.)

If train A leaves the Chicago station bound for San Francisco at 30 mph, gaining speed by 10 mph every 150 miles, and train B leaves the San Francisco station heading toward Chicago at 26 mph, gaining speed by 12 mph every 60 miles, what will enable a passenger on train A to send flowers or buy a gift with a single click on her cell phone for her friend who just called to say she'd had a baby?

a.)   Moore's Law

b.)   InfoSpace

c.)   Snail mail

d.)   The conductor

- People are mobile, and now the Internet must become mobile. InfoSpace provides infrastructure for commerce, information and communication on Internet devices, wireless or not.

- InfoSpace has pioneered innovative and unique services such as single-click purchasing and location-based promotions for wireless devices.

- InfoSpace is a leader in the integration of the Internet and brick-and-mortar commerce. Wireless devices are key to trafficking shoppers to physical locations.

- No other company has actively networked local merchants' business online and in physical stores enabling a new generation of mobile commerce.

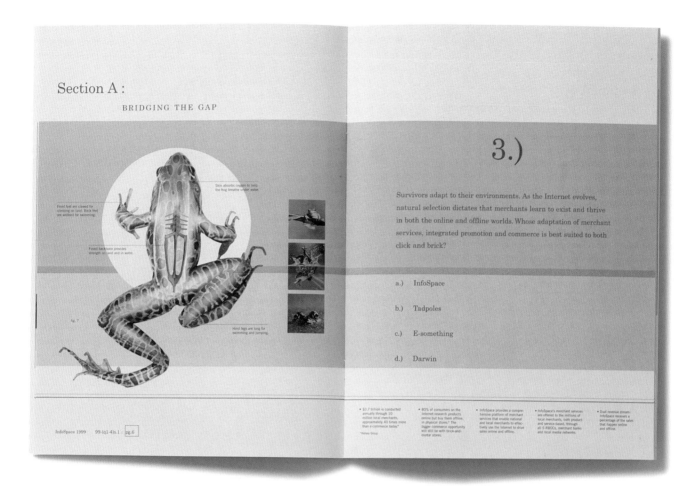

Section A :

BRIDGING THE GAP

3.)

Survivors adapt to their environments. As the Internet evolves, natural selection dictates that merchants learn to exist and thrive in both the online and offline worlds. Whose adaptation of merchant services, integrated promotion and commerce is best suited to both click and brick?

a.)   InfoSpace

b.)   Tadpoles

c.)   E-something

d.)   Darwin

CATEGORY   Annual Report
DESIGN   Kim Napóli
                   Seattle, Washington
CREATIVE DIRECTION Ray Ueno
ILLUSTRATION   Kim Napóli
COPYWRITER   Don Varyu
DESIGN OFFICE   The Leonhardt Group
CLIENT   InfoSpace
PRINCIPAL TYPE   Century Schoolbook
                   and Trade Gothic
DIMENSIONS   8¹/₂ x 11 in.
                   (21.6 x 27.9 cm)

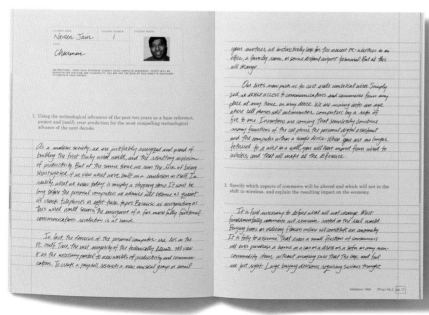

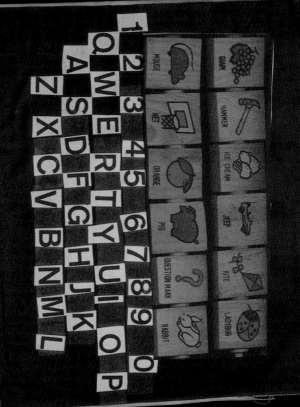

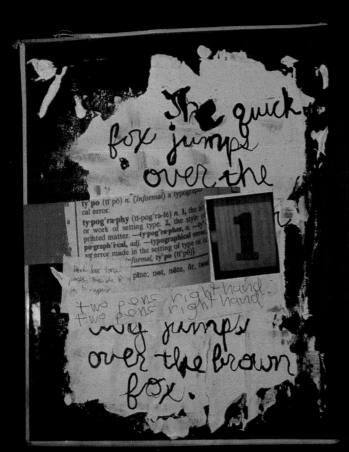

The quick fox jumps over the

ty·po (tī'pō) n. (Informal) a typographical error.
ty·pog'ra·phy (tī-pŏg'rə-fē) n. 1, the art
or work of setting type. 2, the style of
printed matter. —ty·pog'ra·pher, n. —ty-
po·graph'i·cal, adj. —typographical error,
an error made in the setting of type or in
—formal, ty'po (tī'pō)}

1

pine; net, nōte, ôr, tool

two fons right hand
two fons right hand
wig jumps
over the brown
fox.

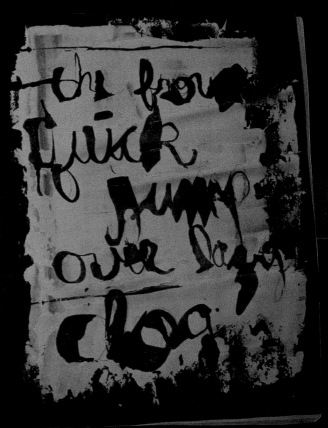

DESIGN Elise M. McDonough
New York, New York
LETTERING Elise M. McDonough
SCHOOL School of Visual Arts
INSTRUCTOR Genevieve Williams
PRINCIPAL TYPE Handlettering and found type
DIMENSIONS 13 x 8 in. (33 x 20.3 cm)

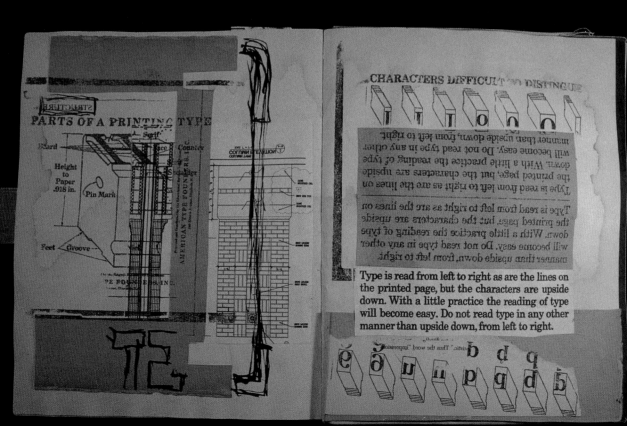

Type is read from left to right as are the lines on the printed page, but the characters are upside down. With a little practice the reading of type will become easy. Do not read type in any other manner than upside down, from left to right.

CATEGORY	Télevision Spót
DESIGN	Marie Hyon
	New York, New York
ART DIRECTION	Kenna Kay
CREATIVE DIRECTION	Kim Rosenblum
STUDIO	TV Land
	(in–house art department,
	MTV Nétworks)
PRINCIPAL TYPE	Entrél and Impacͭt

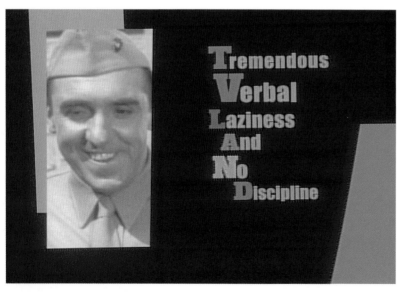

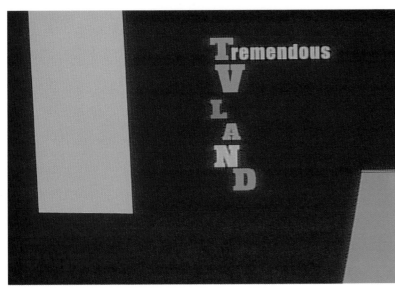

CATEGORY Poster
DESIGN Shinnoske Sugisaki
Osaka, Japan
ART DIRECTION Shinnoske Sugisaki
DESIGN OFFICE Shinnoske, Inc.
CLIENT Shanghai International
Friendship – City Exchange
Projects Promotion
Foundation, Japan China
Art Exchange Association
PRINCIPAL TYPE Kaisho MCBK1
DIMENSIONS 40³/₁₆ x 28¹¹/₁₆ in.
(102 x 72.8 cm)

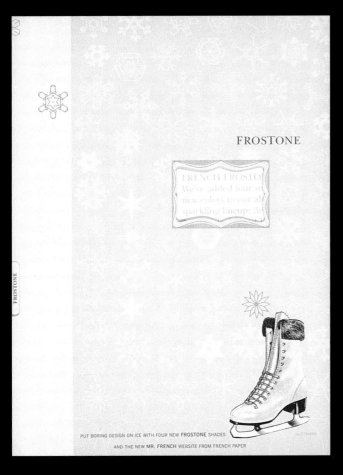

FROSTONE

PUT BORING DESIGN ON ICE WITH FOUR NEW **FROSTONE** SHADES

AND THE NEW **MR. FRENCH** WEBSITE FROM FRENCH PAPER

CATEGORY Brochure
DESIGN Laurie DeMartino
and Paulina Reyes
Minneapólis, Minnesóta
ART DIRECTION Laurie DeMartino
COPYWRITER Lisa Pemrick
DESIGN OFFICE Studio d Design
CLIENT French Paper Company
PRINCIPAL TYPE New Baskervílle,
News Góthic,
Clarendon, and Courier
DIMENSIONS 5³/₄ x 7³/₄ in.
(14.6 x 19.7 cm)

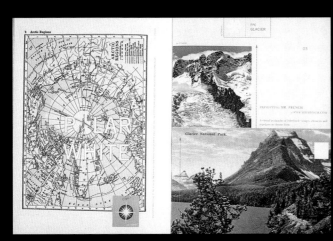

GREATER FOCUS

Curious Corporation Annual Report 2001-3002

CATEGORY	Annual Report
DESIGN	Frank Viva
	Toronto, Ontario, Canada
ART DIRECTION	Frank Viva
COPYWRITER	Doug Dólan and Frank Viva
DESIGN OFFICE	Viva Dólan
	Communications & Design
CLIENT	Curious Paper Cóllection
	by Arjo Wiggins Fine Papers
PRINCIPAL TYPE	Adobe Caslon Regular,
	Univers 53, and Blaćkoak
DIMENSIONS	6½ x 8½ in. (16.5 x 21.6 cm)

LOOKING A HEAD

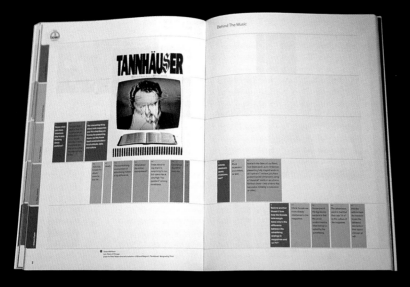

CATEGORY Brochure
DESIGN Rick Valicenti
  Barrington, Illinois
DESIGN OFFICE Thirst
CLIENT Gilbert Paper
PRINCIPAL TYPE Gilbert Identity,
  Akzidenz Grotesk,
  and Adobe Garamond
DIMENSIONS 9 x 12 in.
  (22.9 x 30.5 cm)

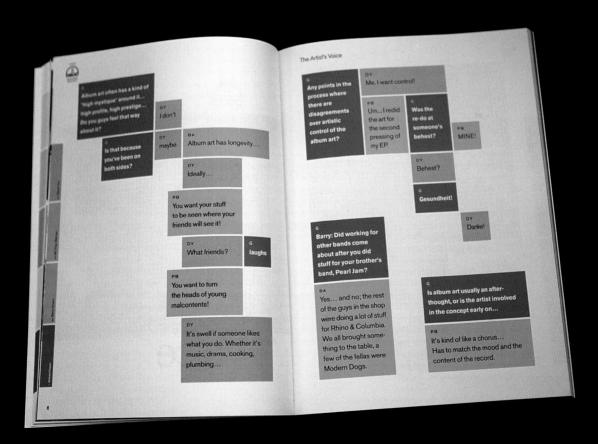

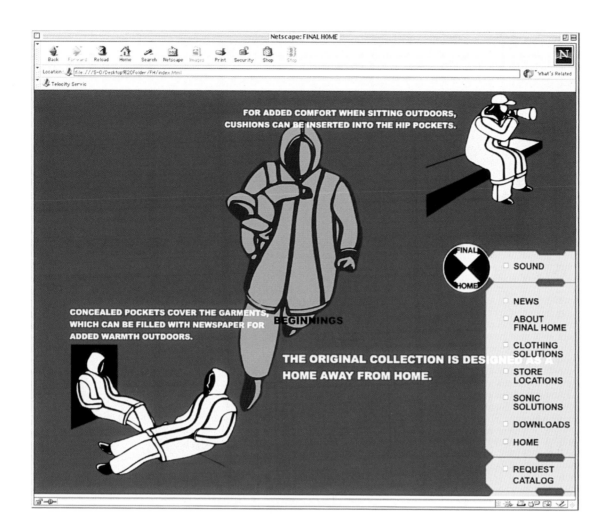

FOR ADDED COMFORT WHEN SITTING OUTDOORS,
CUSHIONS CAN BE INSERTED INTO THE HIP POCKETS.

CONCEALED POCKETS COVER THE GARMENTS,
WHICH CAN BE FILLED WITH NEWSPAPER FOR
ADDED WARMTH OUTDOORS.

BEGINNINGS

THE ORIGINAL COLLECTION IS DESIGNED AS A
HOME AWAY FROM HOME.

FINAL HOME

○ SOUND

○ NEWS

○ ABOUT
FINAL HOME

○ CLOTHING
SOLUTIONS

○ STORE
LOCATIONS

○ SONIC
SOLUTIONS

○ DOWNLOADS

○ HOME

○ REQUEST
CATALOG

CATEGORY	Web Site
DESIGN	Mariko Iizuka
	New York, New York
ART DIRECTION	Sayuri Shoji and
	Nélson Wong
SOUND	ST Sound
STUDIO	Sayuri Studio
CLIENT	Issey Miyake, USA
PRINCIPAL TYPE	Hélvética Neue
	and Arial

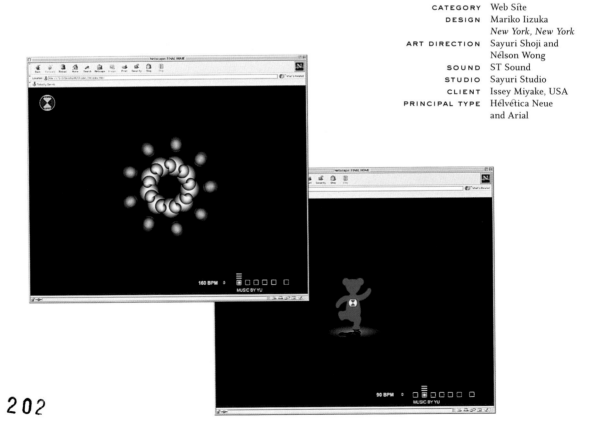

160 BPM

MUSIC BY YU

90 BPM

MUSIC BY YU

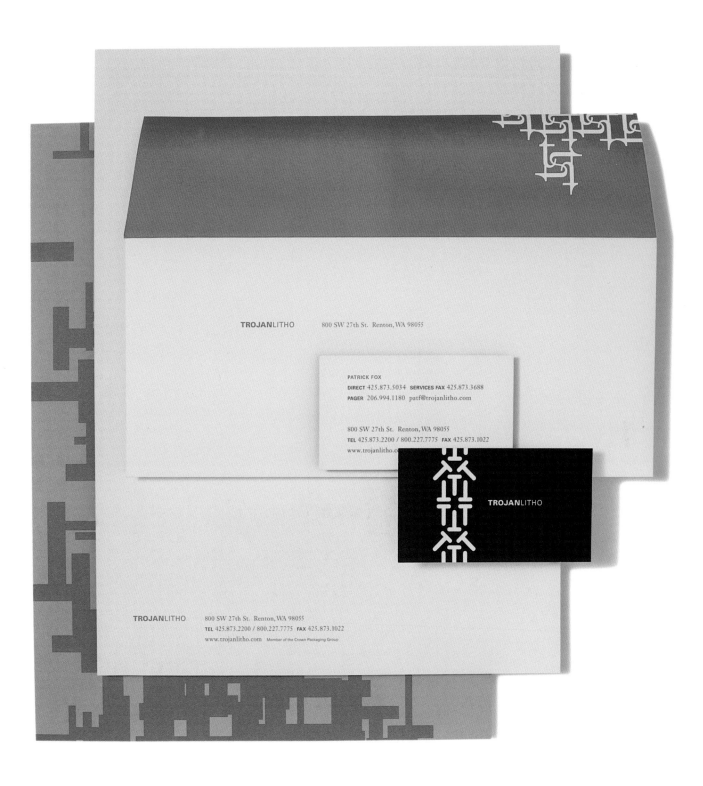

CATEGORY Stationery
DESIGN Misha Zadeh Graham
Seattle, Washington
ART DIRECTION Thad Boss
CREATIVE DIRECTION Steve Barrétt
PRODUCTION MANAGER Diana Frye
DESIGN OFFICE Werkhaus Creative
Communications
CLIENT Trojan Lithograph
PRINCIPAL TYPE Univers, Janson Text,
New Century Schoolbook,
and VAG Rounded
DIMENSIONS 8¹/₂ x 11 in.
(21.6 x 27.9 cm)

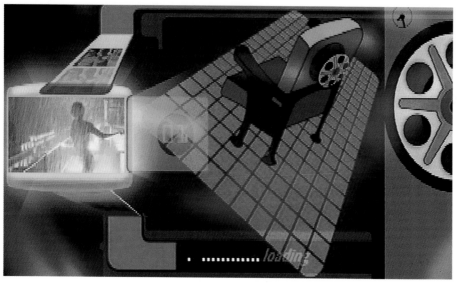

CATEGORY Film Trailer
DESIGN Mark Winn
San Francisco, California
ART DIRECTION Mark Winn
CREATIVE DIRECTION Neal Zimmermann
STUDIO Vehicle SF
CLIENT San Francisco Film Sociéty
PRINCIPAL TYPE Techno, Barmeno,
and Hélvética

CATEGORY	Catalog
DESIGN	Pacey Chao and
	Yu-Pin Cheng
	Taipei, Taiwan
CALLIGRAPHY	Yang Tze Tong
ART DIRECTION	Van So
CREATIVE DIRECTION	Van So
PRODUCTION	Peacock Blue
AGENCY	JRV International
	Company Limited
CLIENT	Yang Tze Tong
PRINCIPAL TYPE	Goudy Old Style,
	Garamond, Inn Ming,
	and handléttering
DIMENSIONS	10⁵/₈ x 10⁹/₁₆ in.
	(27 x 26.8 cm)

CATEGORY Student Project
DESIGN   Julia Hoffmann
          New York, New York
SCHOOL   School of Visual Arts
INSTRUCTOR Carin Góldberg
PRINCIPAL TYPE Góthic 13, Paula Wood,
          and Bembo
DIMENSIONS 9 x 4½ in.
          (22.9 x 11.4 cm)

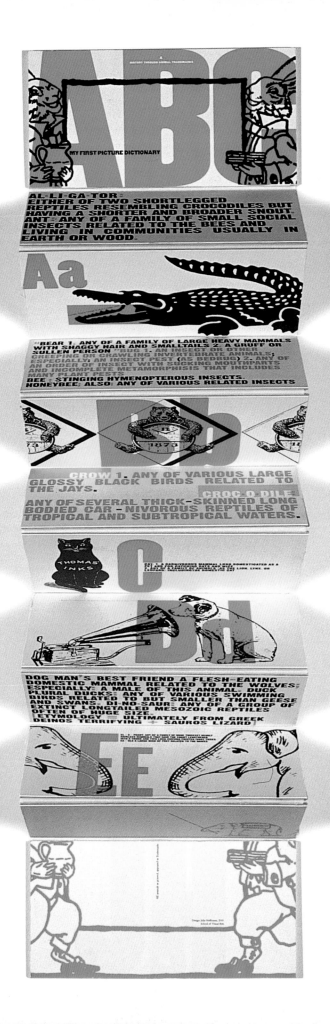

CATEGORY	Poster
DESIGN	Heather Heflin and Paul Gillis
	Seattle, Washington
ART DIRECTION	Heather Heflin and Paul Gillis
CREATIVE DIRECTION	Heather Heflin and Paul Gillis
PRODUCTION	John Lunt
ACCOUNT MANAGER	Kelly Coller
DESIGN OFFICE	NBBJ Graphic Design
CLIENT	Consolidated Works
PRINCIPAL TYPE	Filosofia, Franklin Gothic, and Sucker
DIMENSIONS	24 x 20 in. (61 x 50.8 cm)

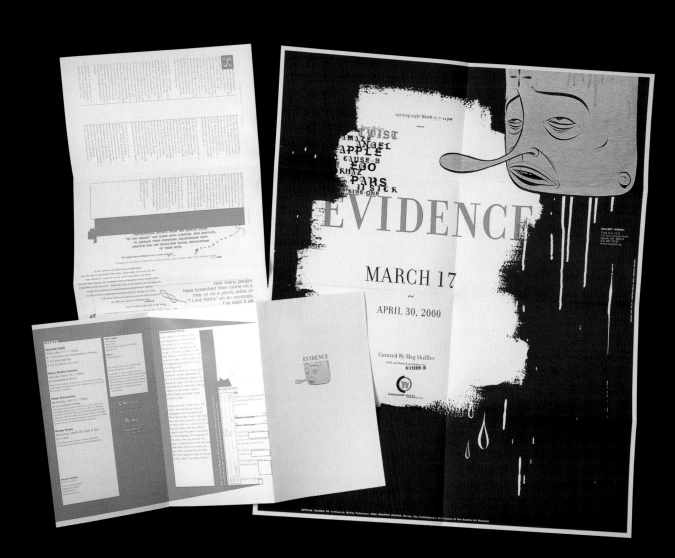

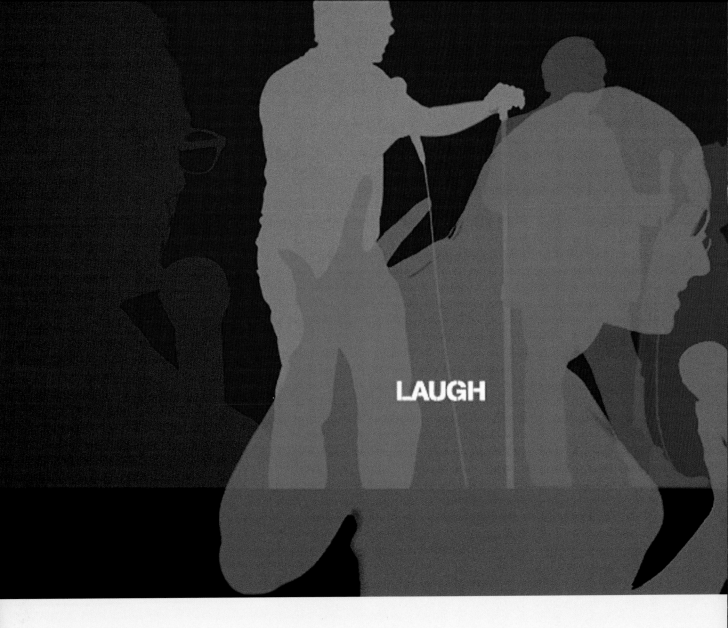

LAUGH

CATEGORY	Show Opening
DESIGN	Vanessa Marzaróli
	Los Angéles, California
CREATIVE DIRECTION	Vanessa Marzaróli
DIRECTOR OF PHOTOGRAPHY	Dan Kohne
ANIMATION	Blake Huber
PRODUCER	Amanda Lehman
EXECUTIVE PRODUCER	Janét Arlótta
PRODUCTION COMPANY	FUƐL
CLIENT	NBC "Late Friday" and
	Ɛxecutive Producer Matt Kunîtz
PRINCIPAL TYPE	AG Book Stencîl

AUGH

LATE FRIDAY

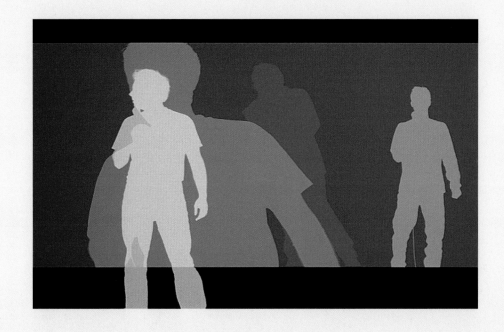

anita giraldo

CATEGORY	Corporate Identity
DESIGN	Ian Perkins and Matthew Gill *New York, New York*
ART DIRECTION	Ian Perkins and Matthew Gill
CREATIVE DIRECTION	Ian Perkins
DESIGN OFFICE	Ian Perkins and Matthew Gill
CLIENT	Anita Giraldo
PRINCIPAL TYPE	Hélvética Neue, Futura, and Bauer Bodoni
DIMENSIONS	Various

ILLUSTRATION Mizue Uematsu
DESIGN OFFICE Flame
CLIENT Department of
Architecture and
Building Engineering,
Tokai University
PRINCIPAL TYPE DIN
DIMENSIONS 5 15/16 x 5 15/16 in.
(15 x 15 cm)

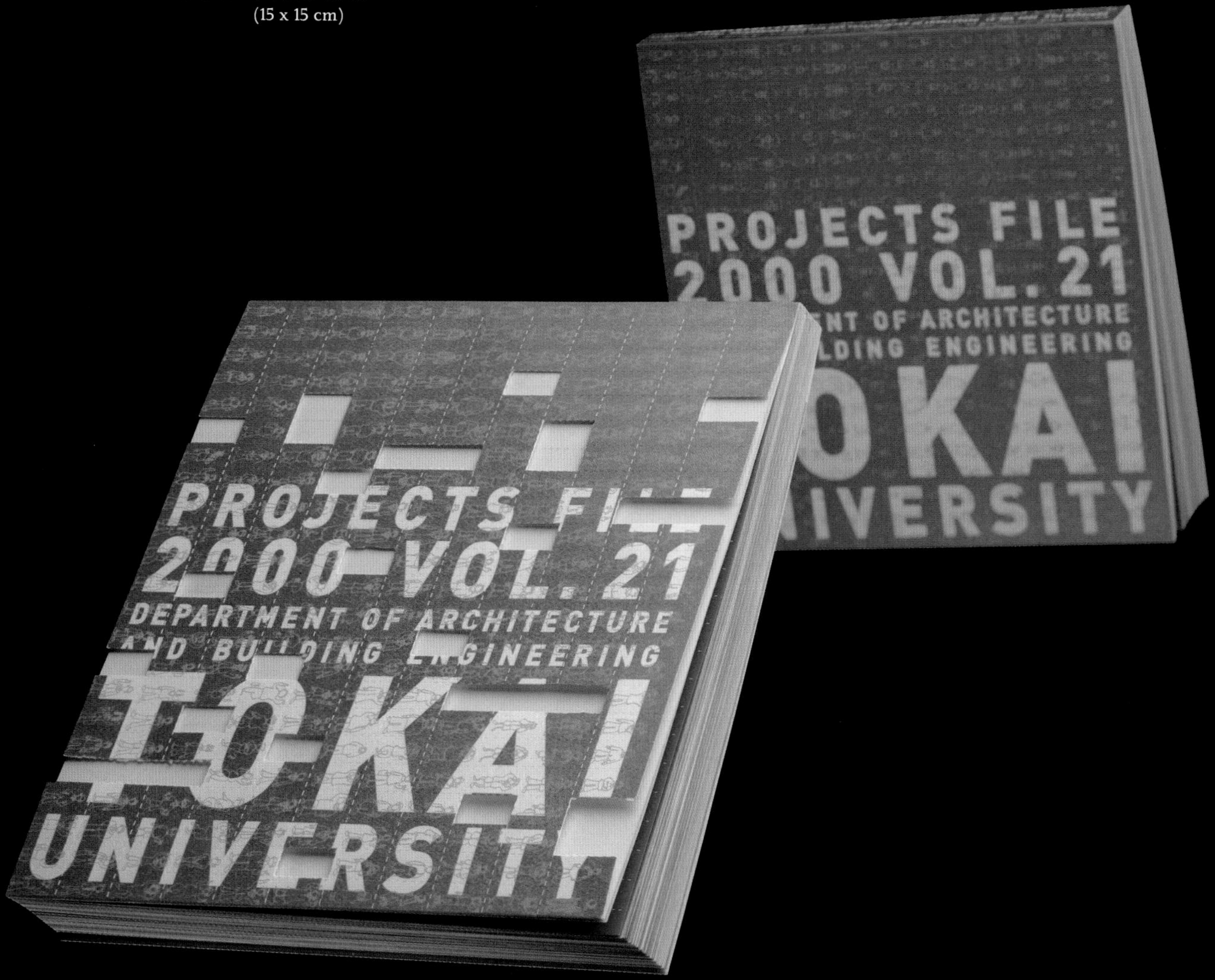

31.12.2000

Ronsdorfer Straße 77a | 40233 Düsseldorf | eMail info@no804.de
Fon 0211.77 92 76-13 | Fax 0211.77 92 76-18 | Leo 0211.77 92 76-19

1 | 1

no.804

DESIGNBÜRO | no.804
visuelle Kommunikation | Köln | Düsseldorf

DESIGNBÜRO | no.804
visuelle Kommunikation | Köln | Düsseldorf

→ ANGEBOT
→ ANGEBOT
→ ANGEBOT
→ ANGEBOT
← BESTÄTIGUNG
← BESTÄTIGUNG
← BESTÄTIGUNG
← BESTÄTIGUNG
↑ RECHNUNG
↑ RECHNUNG
↑ RECHNUNG
↑ RECHNUNG
↓ MAHNUNG!
↓ MAHNUNG!

→ mfg   mfg
→ mfg   mfg
   mfg   mfg
→ mfg   mfg

☼ © ① ① @ €
☼ © ① ① @ €
☼ © ① ① @ €
☼ © ① ① @ €

⚡ FRAGILE!
⚡ FRAGILE!
⚡ FRAGILE!
⚡ FRAGILE!

804   804
804   804

no.804 →   804 →
no.804 →   no.804 →

DESIGNBÜRO | no.804
visuelle Kommunikation | Köln | Düsseldorf

DESIGNBÜRO | no.804
visuelle Kommunikation | Köln | Düsseldorf

DESIGNBÜRO | no.804
visuelle Kommunikation | Köln | Düsseldorf

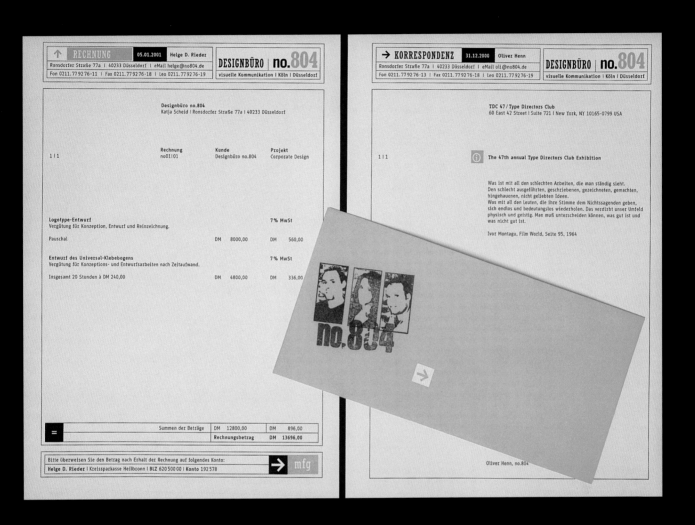

RECHNUNG 05.01.2001 Helge D. Rieder

Ronsdorfer Straße 77a I 40233 Düsseldorf I eMail helge@no804.de
Fon 0211. 77 92 76-11 I Fax 0211. 77 92 76-18 I Leo 0211. 77 92 76-19

DESIGNBÜRO | no.804
visuelle Kommunikation I Köln I Düsseldorf

Designbüro no.804
Katja Scheid I Ronsdorfer Straße 77a I 40233 Düsseldorf

| 1 I 1 | Rechnung no01I01 | Kunde Designbüro no.804 | Projekt Corporate Design |

Logotype-Entwurf
Vergütung für Konzeption, Entwurf und Reinzeichnung. 7 % MwSt

Pauschal DM 8000,00 DM 560,00

Entwurf des Universal-Klebebogens
Vergütung für Konzeptions- und Entwurfsarbeiten nach Zeitaufwand. 7 % MwSt

Insgesamt 20 Stunden à DM 240,00 DM 4800,00 DM 336,00

| = | Summen der Beträge | DM 12800,00 | DM 896,00 |
| | Rechnungsbetrag | DM 13696,00 | |

Bitte überweisen Sie den Betrag nach Erhalt der Rechnung auf folgendes Konto:
Helge D. Rieder I Kreissparkasse Heilbronn I BLZ 620 500 00 I Konto 192 578 → mfg

→ **KORRESPONDENZ** 31.12.2000 Oliver Henn

Ronsdorfer Straße 77a I 40233 Düsseldorf I eMail oli @no804.de
Fon 0211. 77 92 76-13 I Fax 0211. 77 92 76-18 I Leo 0211. 77 92 76-19

DESIGNBÜRO | no.804
visuelle Kommunikation I Köln I Düsseldorf

TDC 47 / Type Directors Club
60 East 42 Street I Suite 721 I New York, NY 10165-0799 USA

1 I 1 The 47th annual Type Directors Club Exhibition

Was ist mit all den schlechten Arbeiten, die man ständig sieht.
Den schlecht ausgeführten, geschriebenen, gezeichneten, gemachten,
hingehauenen, nicht geliebten Ideen.
Was mit all den Leuten, die ihre Stimme dem Nichtssagenden geben,
sich endlos und bedeutungslos wiederholen. Das verdirbt unser Umfeld
physisch und geistig. Man muß unterscheiden können, was gut ist und
was nicht gut ist.

Ivor Montagu, Film World, Seite 95, 1964

Oliver Henn, no.804

CATEGORY Stationery
DESIGN Oliver Henn,
Hélge D. Rieder,
and Kafja Scheid
Düsseldorf, Germany
DESIGN OFFICE Designbüro
no. 804
PRINCIPAL TYPE Rockwéll and
FF Info Office
DIMENSIONS 8¹/₄ x 11¹/₂ in.
(21 x 29.7 cm)

CATEGORY Promotion
DESIGN Masayoshi Kodaira
Tokyo, Japan
LETTERING Masayoshi Kodaira
ART DIRECTION Masayoshi Kodaira
DESIGN OFFICE Flame
CLIENT Japanese Society
of Commercial
Space Designers
PRINCIPAL TYPE DIN Engschrift
and handlettering

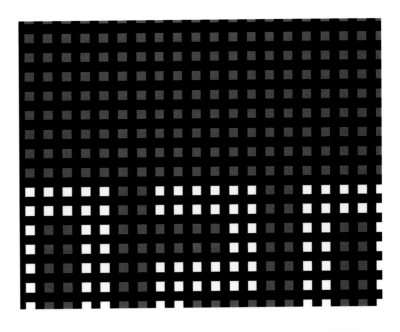

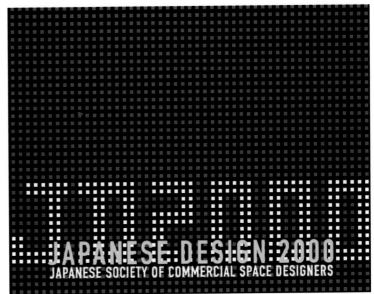

JAPANESE DESIGN 2000
JAPANESE SOCIETY OF COMMERCIAL SPACE DESIGNERS

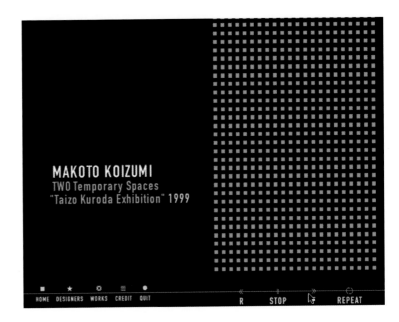

MAKOTO KOIZUMI
TWO Temporary Spaces
"Taizo Kuroda Exhibition" 1999

HOME   DESIGNERS   WORKS   CREDIT   QUIT   R   STOP   REPEAT

CATEGORY	Campaign
DESIGN	Alan Leusink and Brian Murphy *New York, New York*
ART DIRECTION	Alan Leusink
CREATIVE DIRECTION	Neil Powell
DESIGN OFFICE	Duffy New York
CLIENT	MYND
PRINCIPAL TYPE	ITC Johnston, Avenir, and Trade Gothic
DIMENSIONS	9 x 6 in. (22.9 x 15.2 cm)

ESPN CLASSIC PRESENTS: THE DECISION

WHO'S THE GREATEST?

MUHAMMAD

ALI

WORLD HEAVYWEIGHT CHAMPION

Photos © Neil Leifer

vs

DOROTHY

HAMILL

OLYMPIC GOLD MEDALIST

POUND FOR POUND

THE BEST SPORTS PROGRAMMING ON TV

OTHER GREAT CONTENDERS

NICKLAUS or **NAMATH** **STAUBACH** or **STRUG**

ONLY ON **ESPN CLASSIC** **BRING HOME THE HITS**

★ EVENTS NIGHTLY ★

SUNDAY	MONDAY	TUESDAY	WEDNESDAY	THURSDAY	FRIDAY	SATURDAY
REEL CLASSIC MOVIES	BASEBALL	FIGHT NIGHT	COLLEGE FOOTBALL	FIGHT NIGHT	NFL	NHL

CATEGORY   Poster
DESIGN   Dan Richards
Portland, Oregon
ART DIRECTION   Dan Richards
CREATIVE DIRECTION   Steve Sandstrom
COPYWRITER   Dan Richards and
Ray Eldard
DESIGN FIRM   Sandstrom Design
CLIENT   ESPN
PRINCIPAL TYPE   Scanned and modified
antique type
DIMENSIONS   19 x 28 in.
(48.3 x 71.1 cm)

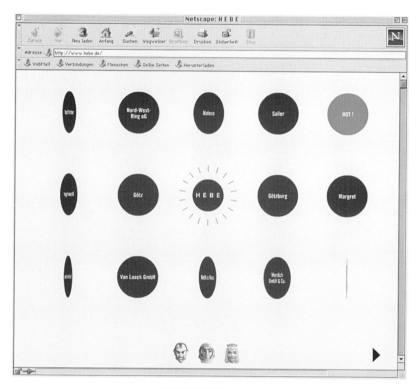

CATEGORY   Web Site
LETTERING   Reiner Hebe
ART DIRECTION   Joerg Bauer
Stuttgart, Germany
CREATIVE DIRECTION   Reiner Hebe
and Joerg Bauer
AGENCY   HEBE. Werbung
& Design
PRINCIPAL TYPE   Trade Gothic,
Clarendon,
and Magneto

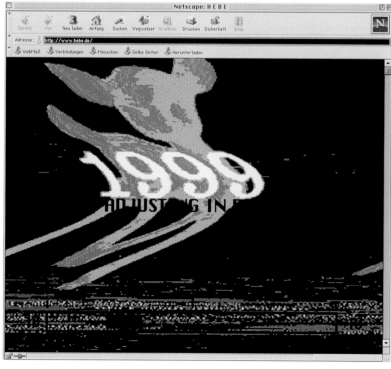

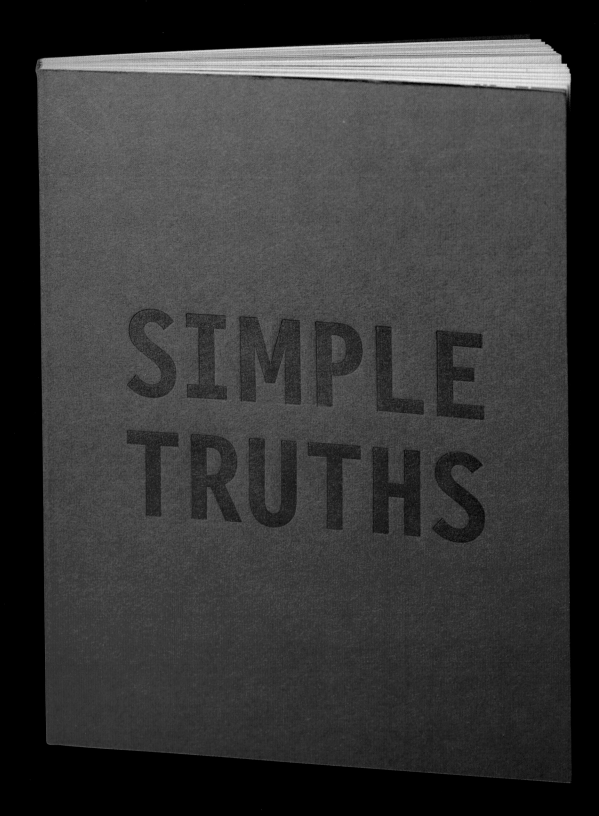

CATEGORY   Annual Report
DESIGN   Marion English Powers
              Birmingham, Alabama
ILLUSTRATION David Webb
DESIGN OFFICE Slaughter Hanson
CLIENT   Greater Alabama Council, Boy Scouts
PRINCIPAL TYPE Helvética, Bell Centennial, and Century
DIMENSIONS   5 x 6¼ in. (12.7 x 15.9 cm)

CATEGORY Editorial
DESIGN Mirko Borsche
Munich, Germany
ART DIRECTION Mirko Borsche
CLIENT Jétzt Magazine
PRINCIPAL TYPE Excélsior
DIMENSIONS 8³⁄₈ x 11¹⁄₈ in.
(21.3 x 28.2 cm)

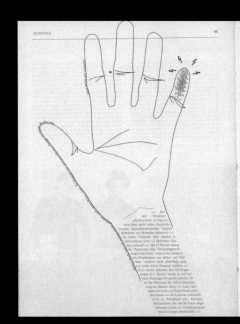

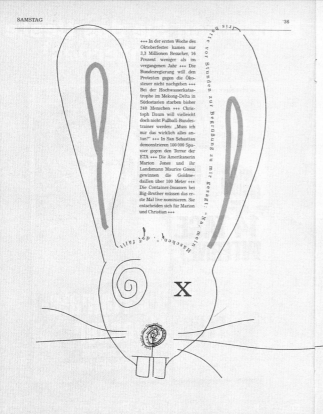

+++ In der ersten Woche des Oktoberfestes kamen nur 3,3 Millionen Besucher, 16 Prozent weniger als im vergangenen Jahr +++ Die Bundesregierung will den Protesten gegen die Ökosteuer nicht nachgeben +++ Bei der Hochwasserkatastrophe im Mekong-Delta in Südostasien starben bisher 240 Menschen +++ Christoph Daum will vielleicht doch nicht Fußball-Bundestrainer werden: „Muss ich nur das wirklich alles antun?" +++ In San Sebastian demonstrieren 100 000 Spanier gegen den Terror der ETA +++ Die Amerikanerin Marion Jones und ihr Landsmann Maurice Green gewinnen die Goldmedaillen über 100 Meter +++ Die Container-Insassen bei Big-Brother müssen das erste Mal live nominieren. Sie entscheiden sich für Marion und Christian +++

¬ENIE VAN DE MEIKLOKJES

Früh um sieben fliege ich von Berlin nach Wien. Im November moderiere ich für das ZDF den Kiddy-Contest, und morgen ist die Vorentscheidung. Als Jury-Mitglied muss ich zwischen 24 Kindern auswählen, welche eine Runde weiterkommen. Am Flughafen holt mich eine Stylistin ab. Sie beratschlagt mit mir, welche Klamotten ich noch brauche, dann fahren wir zum Einkaufen in die Stadt. Einkaufen! Ich liebe das! Ich kaufe mir Schuhe und eine Tasche von Prada. Eine rote. Ich bin glücklich. Am Nachmittag habe ich frei, das passt mir sehr gut. Ich finde Wien wunderbar. In Wien geht alles einen Schritt langsamer, das ist sehr angenehm. Die Leute betzen einen nicht so. Ich habe viele Freunde in Wien. Eigentlich nirgends so viele wie hier. Lustig, dass mir das jetzt auffällt. Ich überlege tatsächlich, irgendwann nach Wien zu ziehen. Habe ich schon immer gewollt.

RAINALD GOETZ

Endlich bricht mir der Schweiß aus, meldet in genau diesen Worten die Fertigsatzstelle im Hirn. Freude entsteht, ich stelle das Sektglas auf die Lautsprecherbox, nehme die Zigarette zwischen die Lippen, fische meinen Füller aus der vorderen, das Notizbuch aus der hinteren Hosentasche und notiere der mir eben hinzutern diktierten Satz. Wir sollen Sekt trinken, nicht Bier, hat Coco gesagt, im Bier wären Östrogene und Müdigkeit, also probiere ich heute mal Sekt. Schmeckt erträglich, nur das Dastehen mit dem Sektglas in der Hand kommt mir so verblödet vor. Ich stehe am Rand der Tanzfläche, im großen, weißen, Moderne-Statement-Foyer des Schauspiels Hannover, die Party ist schon in vollem Gang, kurz vor Mitternacht, ich bin gerade aus der Kantine dazugekommen und wippe mich so langsam rein ins Geschehen. Die neue Mannschaft hier, wie die Züricher ein Ableger der Baumbauerschen Ära in Hamburg, wo meine Theaterheimat der letzten sieben Jahre war, feiert ihre erste Spielzeiteröffnung nicht mit einer ersten Inszenierung, sondern mit einer Eröffnungsparty. Und weil mein Psychiatrie- und 80er-Jahre-Roman „Irre" hier als Stück auf die Bühne gebracht wird, das waren zwei Monate im Sommer, die gemeinsame Arbeit an einer Textfassung, bin ich hier also auch dabei: Lesung, Auftritt, Interview, Party. Es wirkt immer so zickig, wenn man mit Interviews Probleme hat oder macht, aber in Wirklichkeit liegen die Probleme in der Form Interview selber, hatte ich eben meinem Interview-Gegenüber zu erklären versucht. Es gibt ein sehr vernünftiges Selbstauskunftstabu, in Konversation gültig, das einen davor schützt, den anderen im Gespräch allzu direkt mit sich selbst zu konfrontieren, durch allzu direkte Fragen über ihn selbst, ihm das Problem der Eitelkeit dadurch aufzudrängen. Das normale Gespräch geht den Umweg über einen dritten Außengegenstand, deshalb wird so viel wertend über alles geredet, über Kino und Musik, Stars, Fernsehen, Mitmensch, dabei kann jeder sich darstellen, ohne direkt von sich selber sprechen zu müssen. Ein anderes Problem von Interviews ist die Wiederholung. Wie oft darf man dasselbe sagen? Hängt natürlich ganz davon ab, vom Typ, der man ist, vom Beruf, den man hat. Aber allzu häufige und hemmungslose Wiederholungen der selben Aussagen wirken bei fast allen Leuten unschön. Speziell die Speicherform Schrift hat eine quasi automatisch in sich eingebaute Innovationsflicht. Weil der geschriebene Text, anders als das mündlich gesprochene Wort, alt wird, schreit er nach Neuem, jedesmal neu. „Wahrnehmen, nicht Denken: Rausch", höre ich jetzt, notiere es. Ja, ich merke, wie schnell ich betrunken werde, dass ich fast schon richtig tanze, dass das Ich nicht so viel über sich wissen darf, wie es im Interview erfährt, gerade der authentoide Schreiber ist auf Ichblindheit angewiesen, auf das Ich als leere, blanke Stelle, wo der Welteinfall passiert, auf den die Wortfabrik dann reagiert. Iris hatte vor Stunden zur Begrüßung zu mir gesagt: „Na, mein Häschen", das fällt mir gerade wieder ein, als Schickung für diese Party-Nacht, für unser Tanzen.

¬RICHARD KROPF¬

Schiebe Pizza in den Ofen, beschließe, heute einen Sporttag einzulegen und schalte den Fernseher ein. 100-Meter-Finale der Männer. Frage mich, ob es mal einen absoluten Rekord gibt. Muss wohl, kann ja keiner in 0,0 Sek. ins Ziel laufen. Freue mich über diese Erkenntnis und überlege, Rudi Cerne vom ZDF mal anzurufen. Unsere Hockey-Herren spielen gegen die Niederlande. Mit zwölf war mein größter Traum, bei Olympia 2000 in Berlin mit der Hockey-Nationalmannschaft Gold zu holen. Aber mit der lausigen Bewerbung damals sank meine Motivation rasch auf null. Kriege Gänsehaut bei der Florett-Fechten-Siegerehrung der Damen. Schalte aus, das ist mir zu emotional. Meine Freundin ruft an, sie scheint besorgt um mich: „Schnapp doch mal ein bisschen frische Luft!" Öffne das Fenster, beginne meine Plattensammlung zu ordnen und stelle fest, dass da ein bisschen zu viele Leichen rumliegen. Perlen der Popmusik wie „Hello Africa!" von Dr. Alban oder „Nice and Easy" von The Real Milli Vanilli. Vielleicht sind das schon Raritäten, wer weiß. Die Platten sind mein Fotoalbum. Das erste Mal Sex, drei Uhr nachts auf Elba, Liebeskummer (vorzugsweise Leonard Cohen), alles musikalisch untermalt und gespeichert. Ist es eigentlich spielig, einen CD-Turm zu besitzen? Wähle Song des Tages: „Slide Show" von Travis mit dem Vers „It's saturday night and your friends are all out, they never call you, they never call you..." Dumpfe Freudlosigkeit. Muss mal wieder verreisen.

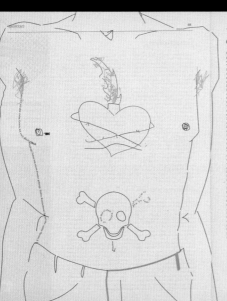

CAROLINE CASARETTO

Heute war unser erster freier Tag, seit wir vor gut anderthalb Wochen ins Olympische Dorf einzogen. Kein Hockey-Spiel, kein Hockey-Training, und was habe ich gemacht? Zwei Hockey-Spiele angeschaut. Es ist nicht so, dass ich mein tägliches Hockey brauche. Nur, im ersten Match, das ich mir ansah - die deutschen Männer gegen Kanada - spielte mein Freund, Christoph Eimer. Und das zweite Spiel, Neuseeland gegen China, zusammen wir uns anschauen, weil wir am Mittwoch gegen China spielen. Ein bisschen spionieren. Mitlaga hatten wir zudem noch eine Besprechung, Taktik und Videoanalyse - doch, doch es gab auch einen Hockey-freien Teil an unserem freien Tag: Am Morgen waren wir mit der halben Mannschaft beim Handball, Deutschland spielte gegen Südkorea. Ich hielt auch sie weiter ein Handballspiel gesehen. Aber die deutsche Handballer wohnen im Olympischen Dorf im Haus neben uns. Hallo Kreiszehner der mit den vielen Toren, hat auch gleich eine zweige Trainings-Fahre aus einem Fenster gehängt. Irgendwann haben wir davon gesagt. Wir kommen mal bei einem Spiel vorbei. Wir sollen auf der Tribüne neben den Handballern, die nicht zum Einsatz kamen, da haben uns versucht, die Regeln zu erklären. Aber ehrlich gesagt, mit Regeln brauchten sie mir nicht kommen. Es war ein spannendes Spiel, die Deutschen haben den Ausgleich bekommen vor Ende geschafft, und die Stimmung in der Halle war umlingend, das hat mir gereicht. Ich überlege gerade, wie die Handballer neben uns höften, Florian, der eine, über den Nachnamen weiß ich gar nicht. Man fragt einen hier ja nie nach Nachnamen. Es zum immel eigentlich nur deutsche Sportler, die wir kennen lernen. Auch wenn wir natürlich schon durch das Dorf laufen und gucken, ob wir jemanden Berühmtes sehen. Ich weiß, unser Trainer Berti Bruch erzählte überall herum, ein, die Mädels waren gespannt, wir im Gustasso-Kurrten gehen haben, den Israelischen Tennisspieler, den finden sie süß. Mein Gott, der Berti. Er weiß immer alles.

"HILLBILLY HOLLYWOOD" WAS AN AMALGAM OF COWBOY AND SHOW BUSINESS, WESTERN AND HONKY TONK, DOWN-HOME, AND LARGER THAN LIFE. THOUGH NASHVILLE WOULD STEAL ITS THUNDER, LOS ANGELES HAD IN THE '40s AND '50s A COUNTRY & WESTERN MUSIC SCENE THAT PRODUCED HIT RECORDS, BIG STARS, AND A STYLE THAT WAS AS GAUDY AS IT WAS ELEGANT.

HILLBILLY HOLLYWOOD

HILLBILLY

H

HOLLYWOOD
BY Debby Bull
The ORIGINS of COUNTRY & WESTERN STYLE

HILLBILLY HOLLYWOOD
THE ORIGINS OF COUNTRY & WESTERN STYLE
BY DEBBY BULL
FEATURING THE VINTAGE COSTUME COLLECTION OF MARTY STUART

224

CATEGORY Book
DESIGN Sharon Werner
and Sarah Nelson
Minneapolis, Minnesota
ART DIRECTION Sharon Werner
AUTHOR Debby Bull
STUDIO Werner Design Werks, Inc.
CLIENT Rizzoli Publishing
and Debby Bull
PRINCIPAL TYPE Hillbilly Hollywood,
Trade Gothic Condensed,
Rockwell, Fournier,
and Sackers Gothic
DIMENSIONS 10 1/2 x 11 1/4 in.
(26.7 x 28.6 cm)

**OFFICIAL SAMPLE BALLOT AND
VOTER INFORMATION**

**GENERAL ELECTION
APRIL 22ND, 2000**

**CLASS NO.150
ART CENTER COLLEGE OF DESIGN
1700 LIDA ST. PASADENA CA. 91103**

A CANDIDATE

Punch the ballot card through the hole
next to the candidate's name

TWO OR MORE CANDIDATES
FOR ONE OFFICE

Punch the ballot card through the holes next to
the names of all the candidates for whom you
want to vote.

FILM FINE ART GRAPHIC DESIGN

018. LEDA, SEBASTIAN   021. CHANG, KIKI
019. SCHILLINGER, ERICA   022. DOOLEY, CHRIS
020. REHMAN, ALIA

LEDA, SEBASTIAN
PRO NAKED LUNCHES   **PRO** PHANTOMS OF LIBERTY
PRO REVERSAL OF FORTUNE
I WILL CANCEL YOUR SUBSCRIPTION TO THE RESURRECTION.

SCHILLINGER, ERICA
PRO CHEESECAKE   **PRO** LA FIESTA GRANDE
VOTE FOR ME. I GOT YOUR TAX CUT RIGHT HERE BABY!

REHMAN, ALIA
PRO SUSHI   **PRO** INTELLIGENT PEOPLE   **PRO** SNUFFILUFFIGUS
NO NEW CILANTRO.

CHANG, KIKI
PRO SILVER   **PRO** NOODLE   **PRO** SUSHI
MORE MONEY TO THE PEOPLE.

DOOLEY, CHRIS
PRO COLUMBO   **PRO** NINJAS   **PRO** PIXEL
RETROFIT THE FUTURE.

P12

GRAPHIC DESIGN

023. DOUGHERTY, SEAN
024. EBARA, SHOKO
025. FOROUZAN, ZHILER
026. GOODMAN, JULIANNA

DOUGHERTY, SEAN
PRO LOG   **PRO** NASCAR   **PRO** SLEEZESTACK
PUSSY COW, PUSSY COW, PUSSY COW.

EBARA, SHOKO
PRO SMILE   **PRO** SAKE   **PRO** SUPERMAN
LET'S HAVE SSS.

FOROUZAN, ZHILER
PRO THE UNTHINKABLE   **PRO** SERIOUS FUN
PRO COMMUNICATION IN IT'S MOST DISTILLED FORM
"NOT WANT TO BE, BUT BEING."

GOODMAN, JULIANNA
PRO SAMBA   **PRO** CHA CHA   **PRO** TANGO
KAKAMAYME.

P13

CATEGORY Student Project
DESIGN Gary Williams
*San Francisco,
California*
ART DIRECTION Chris Dooley,
Sean Dougherty,
and Gary Williams
PHOTOGRAPHY Stephen Franco
ILLUSTRATION Saiman Chow
SCHOOL Art Center
College of Design
PRINCIPAL TYPE Franklin Gothic
and Times
DIMENSIONS 5 1/2 x 7 1/4 in.
(14 x 18.4 cm)

**MEMBERS OF THE
150TH CLASS WHO
ARE CAMERA-SHY**
VOTE FOR NO MORE
THAN FIVE

ENVIRONMENTAL
CHONG, SUNWOO
PULLIAM, AMY
YOON, JENNY
FERNANDEZ, ROHIT
MURRAY, KIMBERLY

FILM
MADZOEFF, MEGAN
MAGANA, JERRY
MENZIES, ANDREW
STRONG, GARY

GRAPHIC DESIGN
CHO, DENNIS
CHOI, ANGELA
COOK, DEBORAH
TAN, ERIC

ILLUSTRATION
CHANG, MEI
GONZALEZ, OLIVIA
NEWSOM, PHILIP
PETERS, COREY
PETERS, ANTHONY
SANDELIUS, STEPHEN
SUNG, SONYA

2	⇒ ○
3	⇒ ○
4	⇒ ○
5	⇒ ○
6	⇒ ○
7	⇒ ○
8	⇒ ○
9	⇒ ○
10	⇒ ○
11	⇒ ○
12	⇒ ○
13	⇒ ○
14	⇒ ○
15	⇒ ○
16	⇒ ○
17	⇒ ○
18	⇒ ○
19	⇒ ○
20	⇒ ○
21	⇒ ○
22	⇒ ○
23	⇒ ○

P36

**MEMBERS OF THE
150TH CLASS WHO
ARE CAMERA-SHY**
VOTE FOR NO MORE
THAN FIVE

PHOTOGRAPHY
BLACK, BETHANY
BOONE, JESSICA
STUDARUS, DAVID

PRODUCT
CHANG, SUNG
DING, WEINA
KUO, WEN
HOSTETTLER, DANIEL

TRANSPORTATION
DOMBROWSKI, RAYMOND
LEE, KYONG
NICOGHOSIAN, GAREN
ZUKERAN, TODD

2	⇒ ○
3	⇒ ○
4	⇒ ○
5	⇒ ○
6	⇒ ○
7	⇒ ○
8	⇒ ○
9	⇒ ○
10	⇒ ○
11	⇒ ○
12	⇒ ○
13	⇒ ○
14	⇒ ○
15	⇒ ○
16	⇒ ○
17	⇒ ○
18	⇒ ○
19	⇒ ○
20	⇒ ○
21	⇒ ○
22	⇒ ○
23	⇒ ○

P37

Portrai
The NSBU Bright Book
3 Co
N
for Small and Enterprise
Businesses
The NSBU Bright Book
NO. 127/150

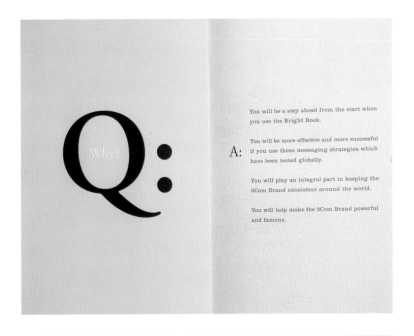

Q: Why?

A: You will be a step ahead from the start when you use the Bright Book.

You will be more effective and more successful if you use these messaging strategies which have been tested globally.

You will play an integral part in keeping the 3Com Brand consistent around the world.

You will help make the 3Com Brand powerful and famous.

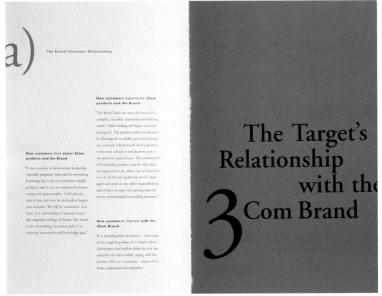

a) The Brand/Customer Relationship

How customers experience 3Com products and the Brand

"The Brand leads me into the future of a complex, stressful, sometimes bewildering world—while warding off danger and minimizing risk. The products make my job easier by allowing me to reliably grow and manage our network. The network itself continues to be more critical to our business and to my personal career success. The combination of brand plus products that do what they are supposed to do, allows me to focus less on I.T. (If I'm not exclusively an I.T. manager) and more on my other responsibilities, and to have an easier time getting approval for my recommended networking purchases."

How customers feel about 3Com products and the Brand

"If you continue to demonstrate leadership (especially pragmatic vision and the networking knowledge that I rely on) and deliver reliable products, and if you are consistently honest, caring and approachable, I will put my trust in you and even be inclined to forgive your mistakes. We will be 'teammates' over time, in a relationship of mutual respect that engenders feelings of loyalty. The Brand is my networking 'insurance policy' to cover my uncertainty and knowledge gaps."

How customers interact with the 3Com Brand

"As a trusted guide, or mentor – with some of the magical qualities of a 'wizard' whose clairvoyance and wisdom helps me stay prepared for the future while coping with the present. Also as a teammate– expected to listen, understand and empathize."

The Target's Relationship with the 3Com Brand

b) Brand Character/Personality

To express the true character of the 3Com Brand, all communication needs to be practical, based in reality, and must demonstrate a personal benefit to the target.

The 3Com Brand personality is based on the following three traits.

Practical
Innovative
(but not beyond the threshold of risking 'safe' innovations for the customer's sake)
Sensitive to needs of growing businesses

Smart
Trusted visionary
Market leader
Intelligent
Confident

Humanist
Mentor
Genuine/honest

CATEGORY   Brochure
DESIGN   Gaby Brink
                San Francisco, California
ART DIRECTION   Gaby Brink
CREATIVE DIRECTION Gaby Brink
                and Joél Templin
ILLUSTRATION   Craig Frazier
DESIGN OFFICE   Templin Brink Design
CLIENT   3Com
PRINCIPAL TYPE Futura, Clarendon, and Garamond
DIMENSIONS   6 x 9 1/2 in.
                (15.2 x 24.1 cm)

PARIHAKA

The Art of Passive Resistance

City Gallery Wellington

CATEGORY	Advertisement
DIRECTION AND ANIMATION	Geoff Dixon,
	Nathan Price,
	Francis Salóle,
	and Paul Freeman
ART DIRECTION	Len Cheeseman
	and Howard Greive
	Wellington, New Zealand
CREATIVE DIRECTION	Gavin Bradley
PRODUCTION COMPANY	Oktobor
AGENCY PRODUCER	Olivia Woodroffe
PRODUCER	Nathan Price
AGENCY	Saatchi & Saatchi
	New Zealand
CLIENT	City Gallery, Wellington
PRINCIPAL TYPE	Pastonchi

230

CATEGORY	Corporate Identity
DESIGN	Clive Piercy
	and Marie Reese
	Santa Monica, California
CREATIVE DIRECTION	Clive Piercy and
	Michael Hodgson
PHOTOGRAPHY	Various
DESIGN OFFICE	Ph.D
CLIENT	Talent Entertainment Group
PRINCIPAL TYPE	Interstate, Mrs. Eaves,
	and News Gothic
DIMENSIONS	Various

CATEGORY	Brochure
DESIGN	Stephanie Wade and Jeff Breidenbach *San Francisco, California*
ART DIRECTION	Stephanie Wade and Jeff Breidenbach
CREATIVE DIRECTION	Stephanie Wade and Jeff Breidenbach
DESIGN OFFICE	levin breidenbach wade
CLIENT	gen art sf
PRINCIPAL TYPE	Trade Gothic and Clarendon
DIMENSIONS	5 x 7 in. (12.7 x 17.8 cm)

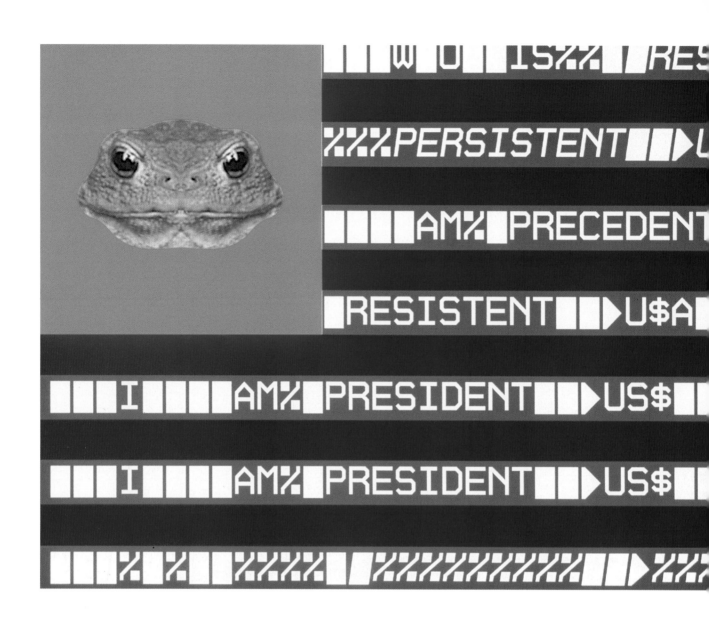

CATEGORY Video
CREATIVE DIRECTION Stephan Walter
New York, New York
AGENCY mass
PRINCIPAL TYPE mass.com

CATEGORY	Manual
DESIGN	Stefanie Tomasek
	Hamburg, Germany
ART DIRECTION	Paul Neulinger
CREATIVE DIRECTION	Johannes Plass
STUDIO	Mutabor Design
CLIENT	Adidas Salomon AG
PRINCIPAL TYPE	Bell Gothic and Trade Gothic
DIMENSIONS	9 1/16 x 12 5/8 in.
	(23 x 32 cm)

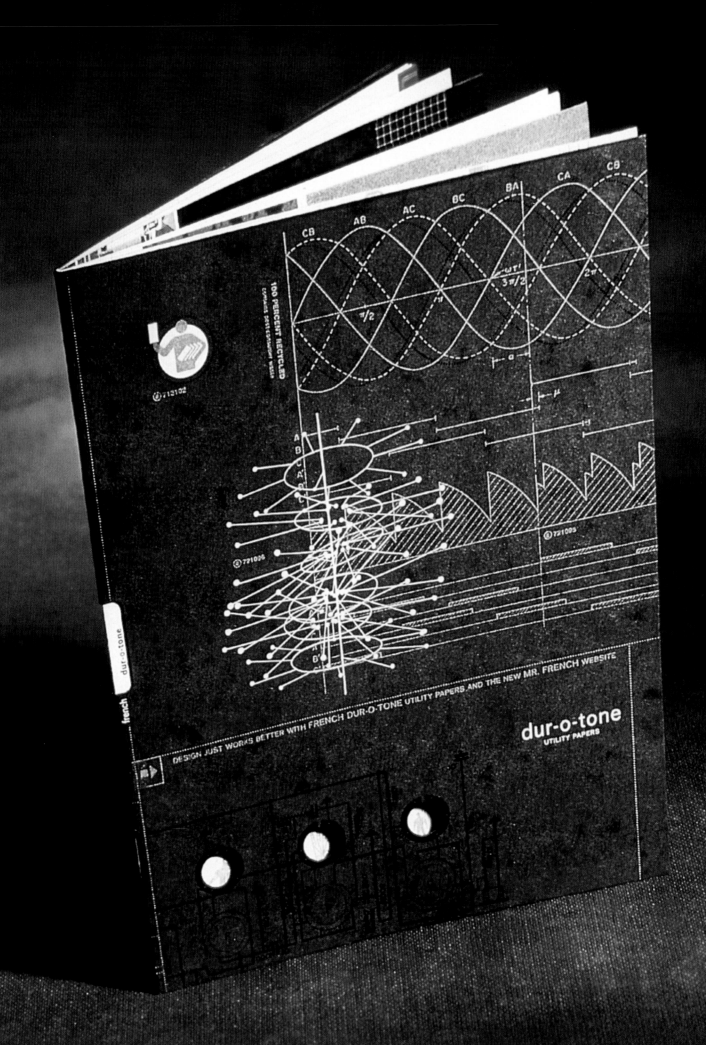

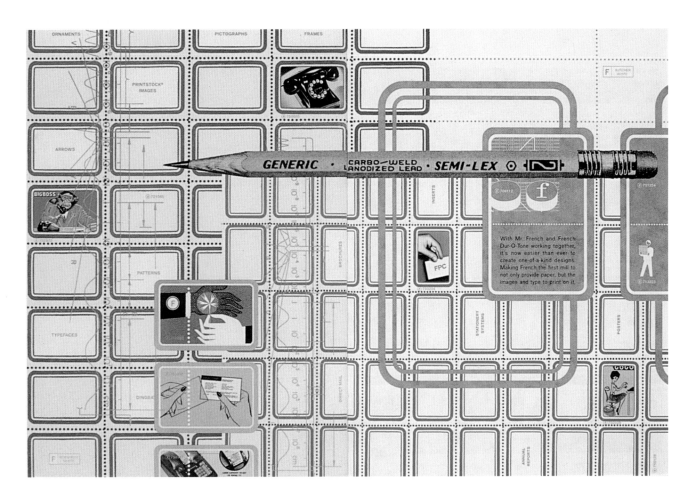

CATEGORY   Brochure
DESIGN   Charles S. Anderson,
Jason Schulte, and Kyle Hames
Minneapólis, Minnesóta
ART DIRECTION   Charles S. Anderson
COPYWRITER   Lisa Pemrick
DESIGN OFFICE   Charles S. Anderson Design
CLIENT   French Paper Company
PRINCIPAL TYPE   Various Mr. French Fonts
DIMENSIONS   5³/₄ x 7³/₄ in. (14.6 x 19.7 cm)

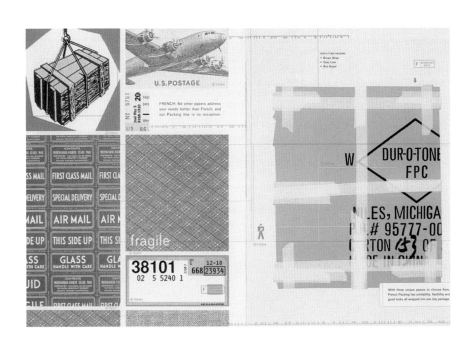

CATEGORY	Corporate Identity
DESIGN	Florian Schoffro and Senta Kock-Bergmeier *Hamburg, Germany*
ART DIRECTION	Pétra Matouschek
CREATIVE DIRECTION	Claudia Fischer-Appélt
AGENCY	Fischer Appélt Kommunikation GmbH
CLIENT	Longhours GmbH
PRINCIPAL TYPE	Trade Góthic Regular, Trade Góthic Condensed Normal, and Trade Góthic Condensed Bóld
DIMENSIONS	Various

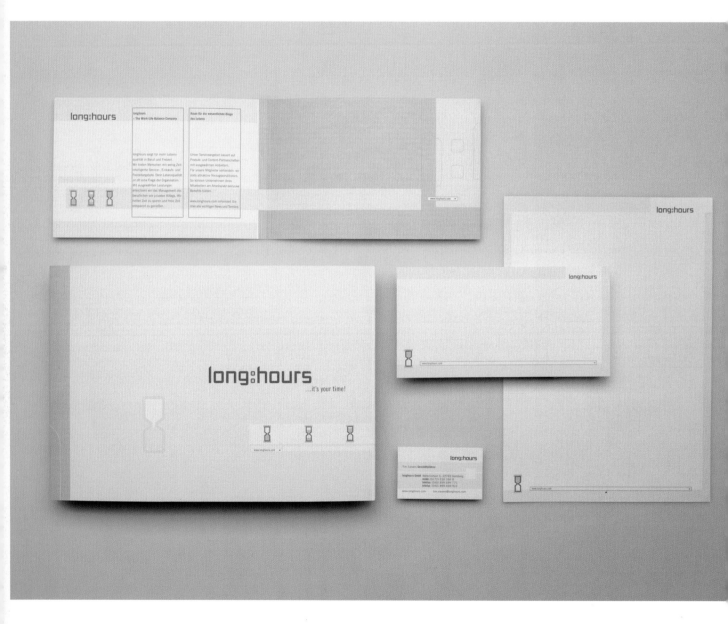

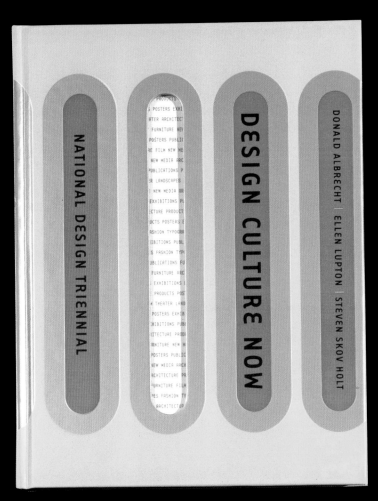

CATEGORY Campaign
DESIGN Ellen Lupton,
Karim Rashid,
Jen Roos, Lynn Yeo,
and Alicia Cheng
New York, New York
CLIENT Cooper-Hewitt,
National Design Museum,
Smithsonian Institution
PRINCIPAL TYPE Filosofia, Tarzana,
and Base Monospace
DIMENSIONS Various

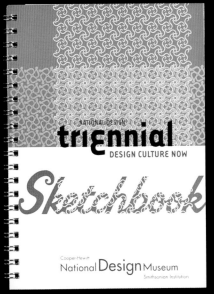

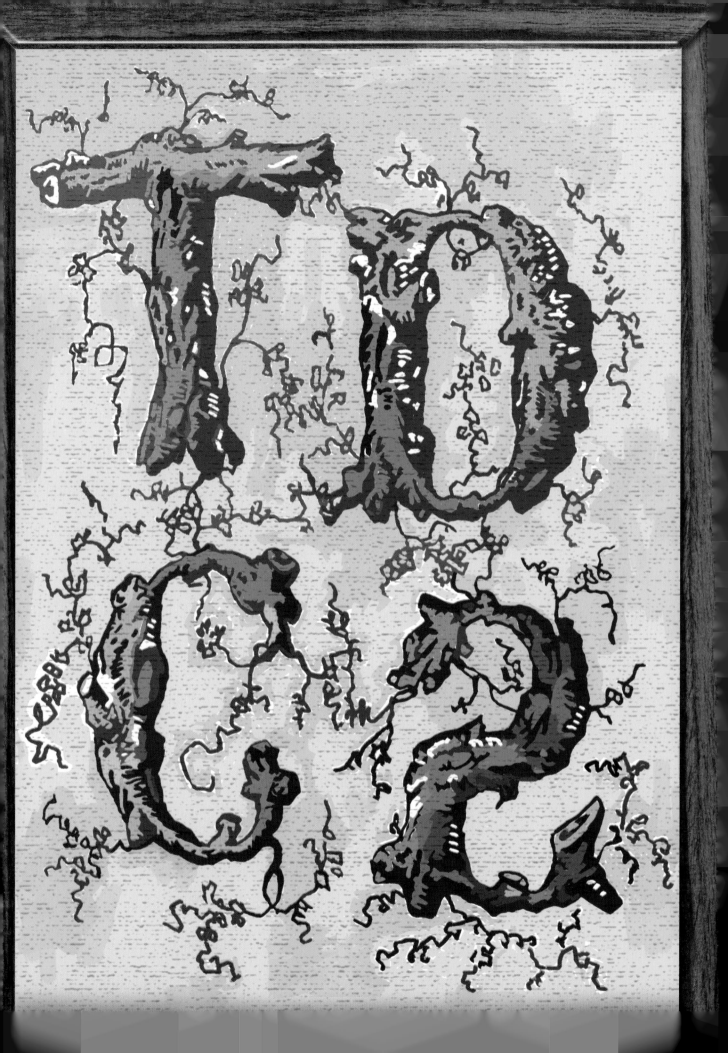

Type
Directors
Club
Typeface
Design
Competition

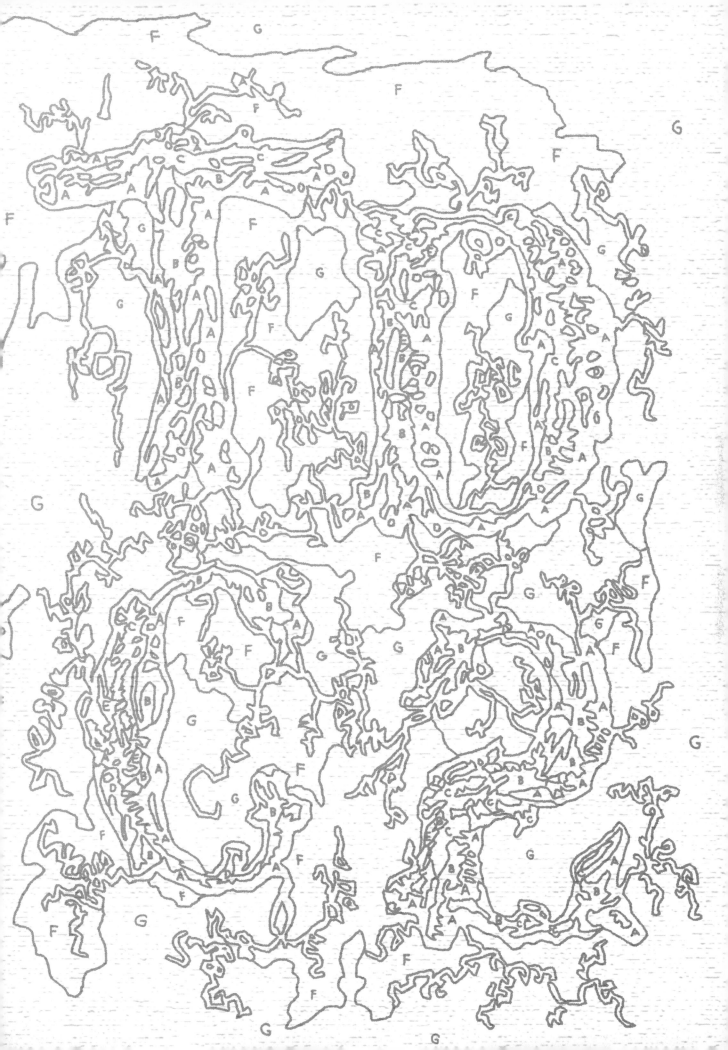

HELEN KEYES

ROBERT BRINGHURST

Judges

TOBIAS FRERE-JONES

CAROL TWOMBLY

NOWHERE is the variety of type design more evident than in the entries submitted to a type competition. From highly distorted novelty faces to subtly modeled text faces in a cascade of weights and styles, every kind of printable letter seems to be alive and well in the modern typographic world At a time when the type business has changed beyond recognition, and when it's not clear how type designers actually make a living at their craft, there seem to be more people designing new typefaces than ever.

One hundred thirty-five typefaces were entered from thirteen countries. The type designs were judged blind; the jury saw no indication of who the designer was or what the typeface was called until after the judging was completed. The winning entries were not ranked, although each judge picked one of the winners as a Judge's Choice.

The four judges of this year's TDC^2 competition (the fourth type-design competition TDC has run) found it easy to make the first cut from the typefaces submitted but pondered a long time over the final decisions of which typefaces to include among the winners. What if a few of the individual letterforms are brilliant but others are not? How do you judge a text face in a language and alphabet that you don't read? How much weight should you give to the way the type designer has chosen to show the face? What do you do with a typeface that's technically well made and works on its own terms, but that you would never use in a typographic design? To resolve one dilemma, the jury created a new category on the fly – "historical revival" – to recognize two well-done digital versions of typefaces originally cut in metal and released many decades ago in Central Europe.

Fourteen typefaces or type families were chosen out of the 135 submitted. The winners represent not just the Latin alphabet but Greek, Cyrillic, and Hebrew; still other scripts were among the entries.

Type design may be the subtlest of crafts, seldom appreciated or even recognized. But the results are used by everyone. TDC^2 honors the practitioners and presents the users with new tools.

Chairman's Statement

John Berry

JOHN D. BERRY is an editor/typographer who works both sides of the design/content divide. He is the former editor and publisher of *U&lc* (*Upper and lower case: The International Journal of Graphic Design and Digital Media*) and of *U&lc Online*. He has a deep and eclectic background in both writing/editing and typography; he made a career for more than twenty years in Seattle as an editor and book designer before moving to New York in early 1998 to take over *U&lc*.

John has done typographic consulting for several software companies, including Adobe, Design Intelligence, and Microsoft; he has written extensively on typography

for such magazines as *Aldus/Adobe Magazine*, *Eye, I.D.*, and *Print*, and writes a regular column on type and design for creativepro.com; and for five years he was the house book designer for Copper Canyon Press, winning several design awards. He is on the board of directors of the Association Typographique Internationale (ATypI) and of the Type Directors Club in New York. He is a founder of Typeset in San Francisco, and he is the U.S. country delegate to ATypI. He lives in San Francisco with the writer Eileen Gunn.

247

Robert Bringhurst

ROBERT BRINGHURST is a poet and typographic historian living in Vancouver. His book *The Elements of Typographic Style* (2nd ed., 1996) is widely used as a textbook and serves as a standard reference in the field. He is also the author, with Warren Chappell, of the newly revised and updated *Short History of the Printed Word*.

THE GRAND DESIGN

1.1 FIRST PRINCIPLES

1.1.1 *Typography exists to honor content.*

Like oratory, music, dance, calligraphy – like anything that lends its grace to language – typography is an art that can be deliberately misused. It is a craft by which the meanings of a text (or its absence of meaning) can be clarified, honored and shared, or knowingly disguised.

In a world rife with unsolicited messages, typography must often draw attention to itself before it will be read. Yet in order to be read, it must relinquish the attention it has drawn. Typography with anything to say therefore aspires to a kind of statuesque transparency. Its other traditional goal is durability: not immunity to change, but a clear superiority to fashion. Typography at its best is a visual form of language linking timelessness and time.

One of the principles of durable typography is always legibility; another is something more than legibility: some earned or unearned interest that gives its living energy to the page. It takes various forms and goes by various names, including serenity, liveliness, laughter, grace and joy.

These principles apply, in different ways, to the typography of business cards, instruction sheets and postage stamps, as well as to editions of religious scriptures, literary classics and other books that aspire to join their ranks. Within limits, the same principles apply even to stock market reports, airline schedules, milk cartons, classified ads. But laughter, grace and joy, like legibility itself, all feed on meaning, which the writer, the words and the subject, not the typographer, must generally provide.

In 1770, a bill was introduced in the English Parliament with the following provisions:

... all women of whatever age, rank, profession, or degree, whether virgins, maids, or widows, that shall ... impose upon, seduce, and betray into matrimony, any of His Majesty's subjects, by the scents, paints, cosmetic washes, artificial teeth, false hair, Spanish wool, iron stays, hoops, high heeled shoes [or] bolstered hips shall incur

Habraam numera
ofaica lege(feptim
naturali fuit ratio
nim Habraam dec
oq; gentium patr
gentes hoc uidelic
:cuius ille iuftitiæ
:qui poft multas
n omnium diuin
:erétur tradidit:ue
n:uel ut hoc quaf
mitari conaret:au
obis modo eft.Po

TOBIAS FRERE-JONES was born in 1970 in New York. An artist raised in a family of writers and printers, he learned the power of written text and naturally slipped into design of letterforms. He graduated from Rhode Island School of Design in 1992 and began full-time work for the Font Bureau as a senior designer. He recently left Font Bureau to return to New York to collaborate with type designer Jonathan Hoefler. To date, he has designed more than 300 typefaces for retail distribution, custom clients, and experiments. At Yale School of Design he teaches a type design course with Matthew Carter.

STRADA
AaBbCcDdEeFfGgHhIiJjKk
LlMmNnOoPpQqRrSsTtUu
VvWwXxYyZz0123456789

GOTHAM
AaBbCcDdEeFfGgHhIiJjKk
LlMmNnOoPpQqRrSsTtUu
VvWwXxYyZz0123456789

MERCURY
AaBbCcDdEeFfGgHhIiJjKk
LlMmNnOoPpQqRrSsTtUu
VvWwXxYyZz0123456789

Retina
AaBbCcDdEeFfGgHhIiJjKk
LlMmNnOoPpQqRrSsTtUu
VvWwXxYyZz0123456789

Tobias Frere-Jones

Helen Keyes

HELEN KEYES is Group Creative Director at Enterprise IG, New York, where she is responsible for the development of creatively powerful and exciting corporate and product brands. Before joining Enterprise IG, Helen was an external consultant to Diefenbach Elkins Davis Baron (U.K.) and Real Time Studio (U.K.); Creative Director of Luxon Carra, London; Senior Designer with Wolff Olins Design, London; and Design Director with Sampson Tyrrell Design. She began her career as a graphic designer with Raymond Loewy International in London.

Monadnock

CAROL TWOMBLY became interested in type while studying graphic design at the Rhode Island School of Design where she graduated with a BFA in 1981. She entered and won first prize (Latin text division) in the 1984 Morisawa Typeface Design Competition with her first original typeface, Mirarae, based on her calligraphy. She became a full-time member of the Adobe type staff in March 1988 and continued there as one of three principal designers until July of 1999. She is the designer of the first three display typefaces in the Adobe Originals collection: Trajan, Charlemagne, and Lithos. She also designed Adobe Caslon, a digital revival of William Caslon's metal typeface family, and several original multiple master families: Myriad (co-designed with Robert Slimbach), Viva, Nueva, and Chaparral.

Carol Twombly

n
u
e
v
a

nueva

abcdefghijklmnopqrstuvwxyz
ABCDEFGHIJKLMNOPQRSTUVWXYZ
¶...+=-\?!,.;#$1234567890&éüiß

Judges' Choices

Designers' Statements

HEBREW, LIKE GREEK AND LATIN, has a rich tradition of pretypographic letterforms, mined to good effect by type designers during much of the past century. The simplicity of archaic Hebrew script (found, for instance, in the Dead Sea Scrolls) has been especially significant in modern design. This type family draws on archaic Hebrew tradition and yet possesses the stylish playfulness typical of much postmodern design. In this respect, it is reminiscent of Carol Twombly's Lithos.

Unlike Greek and Latin, Hebrew has remained a unicameral alphabet: it never developed an upper- and lowercase. For that reason, Hebrew fonts inspired by archaic script can be used in modern time for normal text. Archaically inspired Latin fonts (Lithos, for example) are never quite that versatile. In the Latin alphabet, normal text typography now requires an upper- and lowercase, but, in Latin as in Greek, "archaic" means uppercase only.

While all of us admired this design, each of the judges spotted problems in the kerning table. A number of combinations are kerned too closely. This produces an ungainly sort of shuffle in the running text. Happily, this is an easy problem to fix.

Robert Bringhurst

I STARTED DESIGNING this typeface while I was still a student at the Bezalel Academy of Art & Design in Jerusalem where I specialized in Hebrew Type.

In the early stages, the design was inspired by a few old hand-drawn letters found on a book cover from the fifties, created by an unknown designer. I was fascinated by the angles of these letters, which reflected an interesting attitude about Hebrew letter structure. After simplifying and modernizing the samples, I continued to create the rest of the alphabet and numbers and added two more weights (Maya Light for body text and Maya Bold for headlines use). I added the fourth style (Maya Stencil) to reflect a more dynamic angle. Using the bold weight as a starting point, I cut the characters at some places to create instability and playfulness. My overall aim was to make the Maya typeface simple and quite strong.

— ODED EZER, *designer*

אבגדהוזחטיכרלמסנןסעפפצץקרשת
1234567890
(.;:"'/˜-=+{[]}⟨⟩?!#₪%שׁ*)

אבגדהוזחטיכרלמסנןסעפפצץקרשת
1234567890
(.;:"'/˜-=+{[]}⟨⟩?!#₪%שׁ*)

אבגדהוזחטיכרלמסנןסעפפצץקרשת
1234567890
(.;:"'/˜-=+{[]}⟨⟩?!#₪%שׁ*)

אבגדהוזחטיכרלמסנןסעפפצץקרשת
1234567890
(.;:"'/˜-=+{[]}⟨⟩?!#₪%שׁ*)

TYPEFACE DESIGNER Oded Ezer
*Tél Aviv, Israél,
and London, England*
TYPEFACE NAME Maya
LANGUAGE Hebrew
TYPEFACE FAMILY/SYSTEM Light, Regular,
Bold, and Stencil

POWERFUL AND CONSISTENT RHYTHM is necessary for any display design. A limited set of parts will make the texture strong — but often lifeless. Instead of begrudging such tight restrictions, this designer has turned them into opportunities. While still commanding the eye, the shapes show a playful and inventive strategy rarely seen in this genre. It's hardly a textface (more than a couple of words would be too much, in fact), but it does an admirable job of building a lot with very little.

TWO YEARS AGO I was searching for ideas to design an invitation — which happened to be for my own wedding — when the Russian one suddenly came out of my memory. I tried to figure out where I had seen it, but I failed to locate the book. So I started to work, based only on my blurred and distorted remembrance of the Russian invitation in an ultra-condensed Latin typeface that combined the distinctive flair of Cyrillic and Greek letters with more contemporary features, such as a strict geometric approach to shapes. The result was Basílica, named after the Greek noun used for some important Catholic and Christian Orthodox churches.

—GABRIEL MARTÍNEZ MEAVE, *designer*

Basílica Quadrata & Rotunda

ABCDEFGHIJKLMNOPQRSTUVWXYZ
abcdefghijklmnopqrstuvwxyz
&ÁÉÍÑ áéíñ [¿?¡!] – – – • • • • " " " " "
$ / # 1234567890

I

ABCDEFGHIJKLMNOPQRSTUVWXYZ
abcdefghijklmnopqrstuvwxyz
&ÁÉÍÑ áéíñ [¿?¡!] – – – • • • • " " " " "
$ / # 1234567890

II

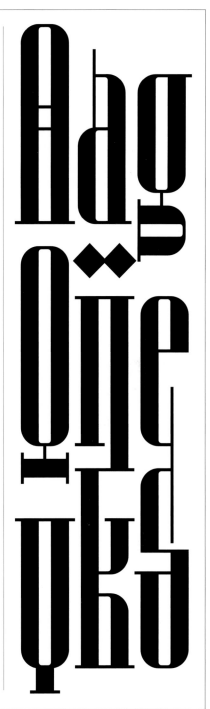

TYPEFACE DESIGNER Gabriél Martínez Meave
México City, México
TYPEFACE NAME Basílica

THIS INTRIGUING PI FONT caught my eye because it was made up of imaginary, smooth, constructed forms, the inspiration for which one can only guess. Having no idea who designed it or the nationality of the creator in the judging process, many of the judges chose this work for its unique qualities. The flange-shape forms and the way these elements were used to create "classic" decorative borders using repeated shapes fascinated us. "Watch parts and tattoos" were mentioned at one point; there is even a surgical appearance to these elements. Even so, in this hi-tech age driven by computers and silicon graphics, it was refreshing to see something created by focusing on pure constructed organic forms and by following where that journey of exploration and imagination could take you. Imagine our surprise when we discovered the creator was Russian!

ZENTRA IS an abstract view of mechanical forms. It discovers new plastic purposes in objects around us. It opens up forms with new characters and a lot of associations. Zentra letterforms may be used in combinations; for example, they make ornaments, fantastic forms, and strong rhythms.
—VLADIMIR PAVLIKOV, *designer*

Zentra

TYPEFACE DESIGNER Vladimir Pavlikov
Moscow, Russia
TYPEFACE NAME Zentra

I CHOSE THIS DESIGN from among the finalists because I was impressed with the interesting detailing that overlays a foundation of consistent, strong, calligraphically based letterforms. The design looks as though it is influenced by early Humanist manuscript styles, especially the Germanic ones. Just as those scripts did, this face in lowercase successfully combines Roman square or versal capitals with slightly "broken" round Gothic shapes. When used in a block of text, this typeface creates a very substantial (dark) color, which may preclude its use for general body copy, though it also has an even, pleasing texture and good readability. Loosely reminiscent of some designs by Rudolph Koch and Oldřich Menhart, this face has a strong personality and a style that I could see using for display and packaging applications as well as for short text settings. I find the italic lovely and the set of small caps nicely proportioned. All in all, this is a very cohesive and well-thought-out type design. And what a wonderful x!

A BIT OF A ROMAN, a bit of a blackletter, a bit of a Fraktur. The late sixties come to mind, the 1460s, of course, with Sweynheym & Pannartz and their letterforms which do not know if they are already Roman or blackletter in style. Then the robust typefaces of around 1900, primarily those designed for private presses. So the Book, bold in its weight, produces a dark text block on the page, preferrably in contrast with splendid white margins. Though lighter and much narrower, the Italic appears in text as dark and so does not stand out at first sight. Additionally wonderful are the long s, some indispensible ligatures, and special figures for paragraph numbering. The name itself is a ligature of *littera atra* — dark letter.

— KARSTEN LÜCKE, *designer*

abcdefghijkl
mnopqrſstu
vwxyzœæöäü

ABCDE
FGHIJ
KLMN
OPQR
STUW
VXYZ

abcdeffghijkl
mnopqrſſstu
vwxyzßœæöäü

ÆŒThthWh
fifffiffifflflfhfk
ffftfftflfflfifffi
ftſſtſpſtſſtſp
ttatutitytwtz
ꝛebꝺꝛepꝺgigrgt

(1234567890)

ABCDE
FGHIJK
LMNOP
QRSTU
VWXYZ

[ÆŒThWh]
ftſſtſpꝛepꝺeꝺ
ttytwtutitzth
ſhfkſlſſlſſſtʃſi
*†‡/«».:?!‚;‹›
ftfftflfflfifffiff
ꝙ1234567890

TYPEFACE DESIGNER Karsten Lücke
Datteln, Germany
TYPEFACE NAME Litteratra
TYPEFACE FAMILY/SYSTEM Book, Italic, and Small Caps

Winners

ENTRIES SELECTED FOR TYPOGRAPHIC EXCELLENCE

TYPEFACE DESIGNER Olivera Stojadinović
Bélgrade, Yugoslavia
FOUNDRY ITC
TYPEFACE NAME ITC Aspera

ITC Aspera

"Imagine
that you have before you a
flagon of wine. You may choose
your own favorite vintage for this imaginary demonstration, so that it be a deep
shimmering crimson in your colour. You have
two goblets before you. One is of solid gold,
wrought in the most exquisite patterns. The
other is of crystal-clear glass, thin as a bubble,
and as transparent. Pour and drink; and
according to your choice of goblet, I
shall know whether or not you are
a connoisseur of wine..."

– Beatrice Warde

TYPEFACE DESIGNER Akira Kobayashi
Tokyo, Japan
FOUNDRY Linótype Library GmbH
TYPEFACE NAME Linótype Conrad™
TYPEFACE FAMILY/SYSTEM Light, Regular, Bóld,
and Extrabóld

LIKE Gudrun Zapf-von Hesse's Alcuin, this is a face that is
neither roman nor italic. It is rooted in older forms — Carolin-
gian forms — that precede the roman/italic split. Nevertheless,
it is thoroughly readable in the present day, and it is pleasant-
ly light-hearted. The light weight seems quite frail, and in the
bóld weight several glyphs (especially M) have grown prob-
lematic. In the middle weights, the lowercase k is the only glyph
that invites revision.

—ROBERT BRINGHURST

The beauty of all typeface lies in its restfulness
and in the way it seems to extract light from thr paper.
This restfulness which makes a type beautiful has nothing lifeless
or paralyzed life. As in the other arts, it consists of a balance of
movement. This calm therefore has two components; life, and
balance or rhythm.
**Harry Graf Kessler in the catalog, Ausstellung von Werken der
modernen Druck und Schreibkunst, Weimar 1905.**

abcdefghijklmnopqrstuvwxyzæœß
ABCDEFGHIJKLMNOPQRSTUVWXYZÆŒ
1234567890.,:;-""''«»*&%/¿¡?!+$£¥§
áàâãäåçéèêëíîïñóòôöõúùûüÀÕÜ

Linotype Conrad™ Akira Kobayashi

Type Design is the basic

The only reliable basic for the design of a type is a positive feeling
for form and style. In order to be able to realize the concept of a typeface, further development until the final type production, requires large
amount of knowlegde and experience. If one wants to achieve the
optimum result of a particular type design, there is neither a design
principle nor any defined production system.

Lino·**tYpE**·Library

THE CZECH DESIGNER Oldřich Menhart was, like Bartók and Cézanne, a master of subtlety and of ruggedness, both at the same time. He designed his Manuscript roman and italic during the Second World War, and the fonts were cut and cast in Prague after the war was over. We were delighted to see a digital revival of Menhart's wonderful face, though disappointed that the revival is so clean. The deliberate roughness intrinsic to the foundry version of the type has here been smoothed away.

All entries to the competition were judged blind, but of course reincarnations of existing types are difficult to miss. For this and another entry — a digital revival of the Preissig type designed by Vojtěch Preissig — we decided to create a new competition category which we called "historical revivals."

—ROBERT BRINGHURST

TYPEFACE DESIGNER Alexander W. White
New York, New York
TYPEFACE NAME Menhart
TYPEFACE FAMILY/SYSTEM Manuscript and Italika

Writers on Writing: Susan Sontag

Excerpted from an article published in The Arts section of the New York Times on Monday December 18, 2000

You write in order to read what you have written and see if it's okay and, since it never is, to rewrite it once, twice, as many times as it takes to get it to be something you can bear to reread. You are your own first, maybe severest, reader. "What is written without effort is in general read without pleasure," said Dr. Johnson, and the maxim seems as remote from contemporary taste as its author. Surely, much that is written without effort gives a great deal of satisfaction. ✿ And though the re-writing – and the rereading – sound like effort, they are actually the most pleasurable parts of writing. Sometimes the only pleasurable parts. ✿ Let's say it's a mess.

But you have a chance to fix it. You try to be clearer. Or deeper. Or more eloquent. Or more eccentric. You try to be true to a world. You want to be more spacious, more authoritative. You want to winch the book out of your balky mind. As the statue is entombed in the block of marble, the novel is inside your head. You try to liberate it. You try to get this wretched stuff on the page closer to what you think your book should be – what you know it can be. ✿

IF TYPE DESIGNERS and typographers could acquire the fame of painters, the Czech artist Vojtěch Preissig would be mentioned in one breath with Oskar Kokoschka and Vincent van Gogh. In 1924 he designed a superbly angular type, cut and cast in the following year by the Czech State Printing House in Prague. Preissig used this type to print an important book of his own, and it came to bear his name, but it was never commercially issued. All serious students of typographic history have seen reproductions of this type, but few have seen it in actual use. We were delighted, therefore, to see a digital revival of Preissig roman and italic entered in this year's competition.

—ROBERT BRINGHURST

TYPEFACE DESIGNER Alexander W. White
New York, New York
TYPEFACE NAME Preissig Antikva and Italika

Egyptian Find Dates Alphabet In Earlier Era

NYT Sunday, November 14, 2000

'This is fresh meat for the alphabet people'

By JOHN NOBLE WILFORD

On the track of an ancient road in the desert west of the Nile, where soldiers, couriers and traders once traveled from Thebes to Abydos, Egyptologists have found limestone inscriptions that they say are the earliest known examples of alphabetic writing. ☞ Their discovery is expected to help fix the time and place for the origin of the alphabet, one of the foremost innovations of civilization. ☞ Carved in the cliffs of soft stone, the writing, in a Semitic script with Egyptian influences, has been dated to somewhere between 1900 and 1800 B.C., two or three centuries earlier than previously recognized uses of a nascent alphabet. The first experiments with an alphabet thus appeared to be the work of Semitic people living deep in Egypt, not in their homelands in the Syria-Palestine region, as had previously been thought. ☞ Although the two inscriptions have yet to be translated, other evidence at the discovery site supports the idea of the

Wadi el-Hol

alphabet as an invention by workaday people that simplified and democratized writing. ✦ Alphabetic writing emerged as a shorthand by which about thirty symbols, each one representing a single sound, could be combined to form words for a wide variety of ideas. This replaced writing systems like hieroglyphics in which hundreds of pictographs, or idea images, had to be mastered. ✦ Dr. John C. Darnell, an Egyptologist at Yale University, and his wife, a Ph.D. student in Egyptology, made the find while conducting a survey of ancient travel routes in the desert of southern Egypt, near the royal city of Thebes and beyond the Pharaoh's tombs in the Valley of the Kings. The Darnells came upon limestone walls marked with grafitti at the forlorn Wadi el-Hol, roughly translated as *Gulch of Terror*. ✦ The next oldest evidence for an alphabet, dated around 1600 B.C., was found in Semitic-speaking territory in the Sinai Peninsula and farther north in the region of the ancient Canaanites. Scholars assumed that Semites developed the alphabet by simplifying Egyptian hieroglyphics, but did it in their own lands. ✦ Surveying the site, the Darnells found an inscription in non-alphabetic Egyptian that started with the name of a certain BEBI, who called himself "general of the Asiatics." ✦

ABCDEFGH
OPQRSTU

a b c d e f g
n o p q r s t u

1 2 3

7 8 9

$ %

TYPEFACE DESIGNER Michaél Lee
Atlanta, Georgia
TYPEFACE NAME Terminator

TYPEFACE DESIGNER	Yvonne Diedrich
	Vienna, Austria
FOUNDRY	Letraset
TYPEFACE NAME	Eplica
TYPEFACE FAMILY/SYSTEM	Eplica Book, Book Italic,
	Book SC, Book SC Italic
	Book Extras:
	Ornament and Ligatures
	Eplica Medium, Medium Italic,
	Medium SC, Medium SC Italic
	Medium Extras:
	Ornaments and Ligatures
	Eplica Bold, Bold Italic,
	Bold SC, Bold SC Italic
	Bold Extras:
	Ornaments and Ligatures

Eplica ↄ

A B C D E F G H I J K L M N O P Q R S T U V W X Y Z a b c d e f g
i j k l m n o p q r s t u v w x y z A B C D E F G H I J K L M N O P Q R S T
U W X Y Z ck ct el et ff fi ffi fl ffl il it ol ot ph pl sl sp st ß ∽ ∾ ↄ
✳✳✳ ∾ ↄ ∾ ∽ 1 2 3 4 5 6 7 8 9 0 1 2 3 4 5 6 7 8 9 0 ½ ¼ ¾
( ) [ ] { } | * @ † ‡ § ¶ & ? ¿ ! ¡ £ $ ¢ ¥ ƒ € ‰ / , ; . : " " " ' ' + × ÷ = - – — _

Eplica ↄ

A B C D E F G H I J K L M N O P Q R S T U V W X Y Z a b c d e f g
i j k l m n o p q r s t u v w x y z A B C D E F G H I J K L M N O P Q R S T U
w x y z ck ct el et ff fi ffi fl ffl il it ol ot ph pl sl sp st ß ∽ ∾ ↄ
✳✳✳ ∾ ↄ ∾ ∽ 1 2 3 4 5 6 7 8 9 0 1 2 3 4 5 6 7 8 9 0 ½ ¼ ¾
*( ) [ ] { } | * @ † ‡ § ¶ & ? ¿ ! ¡ £ $ ¢ ¥ ƒ € ‰ / , ; . : " " " ' ' + × ÷ = - – — _*

Eplica_Text Family [17 POINT TEXT] bilateral serif construction
Reflection of – typographic chronology / «*historical travelling*»
Old Face & Modern Face style [book, medium, bold] - LETRASET.COM

"I'M REALLY NOT SURE what use this typeface would find in the "real world," but with that concern set aside, this is a really impressive piece of work. It starts with an absurdly tall order — a monospaced, single-height roman/blackletter hybrid — and completes it with surprising success.

—TOBIAS FRERE-JONES

TYPEFACE DESIGNER	Rie Amaki
	Pasadena, California
INSTRUCTOR	Jens Gehlhaar
SCHOOL	Art Center College of Design
TYPEFACE NAME	Hierarchy
TYPEFACE FAMILY/SYSTEM	Light, Regular, and Bold

&=❋❖❉

QWERTYUIOP[{}]""

ASDFGHJKL;:789

ZÆCVBNM/?456

123

0

qwertyuiop 789

qwertyuiopasdfghjkl789456

asdfghjklzæcvbnm 456123

zæcvbnm 1230

0

HIERARCHY

is based on karl marx's idea of equality.
HIERARCHY breaks all the class rules of typefaces: uppercase,
lowercase, numerals, punctuations, serif, and sanserif.
each letter is treated equally, much like karl marx's idea.

 monospace·monoweight·semiserif·uniheight

TYPEFACE DESIGNER Gary Munch
                   Stamford, Connecticut
         FOUNDRY   Linotype Library
   TYPEFACE NAME   Really Cyrillic & Really Greek
       LANGUAGE   Cyrillic and Greek
TYPEFACE FAMILY/SYSTEM Really Cyrillic: Medium, Demibóld,
                        Medium Italic, and Demibóld Italic
                        Really Greek: Medium, Demibóld,
                        Medium Italic, and Demibóld Italic

Νομίζω ότι είναι ιδιαίτερα

Я думаю, довольно трудно

δύσκολο να δημιουργηθεί μια

создать новый рисунок

καινούργια γραμματοσειρά,

шрифта, или, раз уж на то

όπως είναι δύσκολο να

пошло, вообще что-либо

δημιουργηθεί ένα καινούργιο ο,

новое для повседневного

τιδήποτε που χρησιμοποιείται

обихода.

καθημερινά.   **Really**

Really Cyrillic and Greek extensions to Linotype Really · Gary Munch

279

MOST DIGITAL FONTS FOLLOW a painfully simple architectural plan which hampers multilingual composition and discourages typographic sophistication even within the bounds of normal English text. Newer and more complex font structures — known in the trade as GX fonts and OpenType fonts — have done much to solve these problems. Warnock Pro, with its large and multilayered character set, is designed on such a groundplan. There are upright and cursive forms of four alphabets (Latin, Greek, Cyrillic, and Latin small caps), together with a large selection of accented characters, swash characters, ligatures, and ornaments. These character sets are drawn in sixteen versions: four weights in four paradigmatic sizes, called caption, text, subhead, and display (based on 8, 12, 18, and 72 point standards).

Overall, the design has a pleasing quality of sharpness and of tautness, mildly reminiscent of bow and arrow or blackberry bush. The sharp terminals of a, c, f, and r in the roman and the thornlike serifs in the italic lowercase all contribute to this effect. Thorniness may sound like an objectionable feature in a typeface, but it is one of several strategies type designers have used to combat the dismal flatness that is typical of text pages printed on a high-speed offset press. In my opinion, the Latin and Cyrillic members of this family are more graceful and successful than the Greek.

—ROBERT BRINGHURST

Warnock Pro

is a new type composition family named after Adobe Systems co-founder, John Warnock, whose visionary spirit led to major advances in desktop publishing and graphic arts software. Warnock Pro is a highly readable and serviceable family, built upon sound principles of classical design while being strongly centered in our time. As a full-featured OpenType family, with Latin, Cyrillic, and Greek character sets in a variety of weights and optical size ranges, Warnock Pro is truly a state-of-the-art composition family that performs a wide variety of typographic tasks with quiet elegance. Its contemporary design and classical appeal lends documents an air of modernity and sophistication.

Caption Light ◆ Caption Regular ◆ **Caption Semibold** ◆ **Caption Bold** ◆ *Caption Light Italic* ◆ *Caption Regular Italic* ◆ ***Caption Semibold Italic*** ◆ ***Caption Bold Italic*** ◆ Text Light ◆ Text Regular ◆ **Text Semibold** ◆ **Text Bold** ◆ *Text Light Italic* ◆ *Text Regular Italic* ◆ ***Text Semibold Italic*** ◆ ***Text Bold Italic*** ◆ Subhead Light ◆ Subhead Regular ◆ **Subhead Semibold** ◆ **Subhead Bold** ◆ *Subhead Light Italic* ◆ *Subhead Regular Italic* ◆ ***Subhead Semibold Italic*** ◆ ***Subhead Bold Italic*** ◆ Display Light ◆ Display Regular ◆ **Display Semibold** ◆ **Display Bold** ◆ *Display Light Italic* ◆ *Display Regular Italic* ◆ ***Display Semibold Italic*** ◆ ***Display Bold Italic***

TYPEFACE DESIGNER Robert Slimbach
San Jose, California
FOUNDRY Adobe Systems, Inc.
TYPEFACE NAME Warnock Pro
LANGUAGE Latin, Greek, Cyrillic

Dept. _____

ame _____

ept. _____

Name _____

Dept. _____

Name MEMBERS _____

Dept. _____

Name _____

Dept. _____

Name _____

Dept. _____

Name _____

Dept. _____

Dept. _____

Name _____

Dept. _____

Name _____

Dept. _____

Name _____

Dept. _____

Name _____

Dept. _____

Name _____

Dept. _____

Name _____

Dept. _____

A	Jaques Bagios 11/7/95	Anna Berkenbusch 1/1/89	Patricia Bradbury 10/25/93	Casandra Calo 5/7/98	Heung-Heung Chin 7/21/98	Madeleine Corson 11/5/96	Bill Dawson 4/2/2001	Pascale Dovic 11/6/97	Rafael Esquer 1/31/2000
Marcella Accardi 4/2/98 s	Peter Bain 1/1/86	John Berry 11/5/96	Fred Brady 1/1/97	Ronn Campisi 1/1/88	Kai-Yan Choi 1/1/90	Susan Cotler-Block 1/1/89	Einat Lisa Day 2/4/97 s	Stephen Doyle 1/29/98	Joseph Michael Essex 1/1/78
Shana Leigh Acosta 7/17/2000 s	Boris Balant 6/30/99	Peter Bertolami 1/1/69 l	Bud Braman 9/18/90	Diane Carrier 10/25/99	Stanley Church 8/14/97	Freeman (Jerry) Craw 1/1/47 l	Josanne DeNatale 1/1/86	John Dreyfus 1/1/68 h	Leslie Evans 3/1/92
Debbie Adams 9/10/98	Marco Balecke 8/23/2000	Davide Bevilacqua 1/7/99	Ulrike Brenner 10/25/99	Matthew Carter 1/1/88	Traci Churchill 5/16/95	Juan Jose Gimeno Crespo 1/19/2001	Roberto deVicqde-Cumptich 8/14/97	Christopher Dubber 1/1/85	Florence Everett 1/1/89
Eric Alb 11/5/96	Bruce Balkin 12/1/92	Tad Biernot 7/17/2000	Ed Brodsky 1/1/80	Tony Castellano 2/4/97	John Clarke 6/18/2001	Laura Crookston 5/8/2000	Matej Decko 10/25/93	Simon Dwelly 9/10/98	Daniel Ewer 7/17/2000
Jack Anderson 6/24/96	Kevin Balluff 1/7/99	Klaus Bietz 8/12/93	Peter Bruhn 11/6/2000	Sergio Castro 5/3/2001	Travis Cliett 1/1/53 l	Bart Crosby 6/21/95	Richard F.Dendy 12/11/2000	Lutz Dziarnowski 1/1/92	
Martyn Anstice 7/28/92	Stephen Banham 9/12/95	Henrik Birkvig 6/24/96	Andreas Brunglinghaus 5/6/97	Ken Cato 1/1/88	Graham Clifford 7/21/98	Ray Cruz 12/6/99	Margi Denton 9/21/99	Lasko Dzurovski 4/4/2000	**F**
Magnus Arason 8/23/2000	Neil Barnett 3/1/2001	Roger Black 1/1/80	Bill Bundzak 1/1/64 l	Paul Caullett 4/2/98 s	Tom Cocozza 1/1/76	Jeff Culver 11/6/97 s	Ernst Dernehl 1/1/87		Peter Fahrni 8/12/93
Don Ariev 4/2/98	David Barrineau s	Alan Boarts 11/5/96	Ulrich Burgdorf 11/5/96	Henrique Cayatte 1/19/2001	Lisa Cohen 2/7/95	David Cundy 1/1/85	Cara Determan 11/6/2000 s	**E**	John Fairley 1/31/2000
Philipp Arnold 11/6/2000 s	Barbara Baumann 9/20/96	Barbara A. Boccio 9/21/99	Queenie Burns 9/20/94	Eric Chan 8/14/97	Stuart Cohen 6/24/96	Brian Cunningham 9/20/96	Meir Deutsch 1/31/2000	Brian Edlefson 1/19/2001	Simon Fairweather 6/18/2001
Pamela Arnold 1/19/2001	Gerd Baumann 6/21/95	Karlheinz Boelling 1/1/86	Thomas F. Burroughs 1/31/2000	Leslie Chan 1/19/2001	Angelo Colella 1/1/90	Rick Cusick 1/1/89	W.Brian Diecks 9/10/98	Friedrich Eisenmenger 8/12/93	John Falker 5/8/2000
Jenna Ashley 11/6/97	Clarence Baylis 1/1/74 l	Garrett Boge 1/1/83	Steve Byers 1/29/98	Theseus Chan 9/20/94	Remle Colestock 8/23/2000 s		A. Claude Dieterich 1/1/84	Jeani Eismont 6/24/96	David Farey 11/30/93
Jeffrey Austin 3/5/98	Chris Bean 4/4/2000	Matteo Bologna 1/31/2000	Patricia Byrnes 4/2/2001	Virginia Chan 11/6/2000	Ed Colker 1/1/83	**D**	Kirsten Dietz 12/11/2000	Lise Ellingson 7/21/98 s	Michael Farmer 7/11/94
	Syndi Becker 6/24/96	John Bonadies 6/21/95		KaiPing Chao 1/19/2001	David Cooke 3/1/2001	Michael Damare 7/21/98	Joseph DiGioia 3/8/99	Dr.Elsi Vassdal Ellis 2/23/93	Erik Faulhaber 11/6/97 s
B	Felix Beltran 1/1/88	Gianni Bortolotti 5/7/98	**C**	David Chaves 11/5/96	Nick Cooke 1/19/2001	Ziya Danishmend 1/31/2000	Tom Dolle 6/21/95	Garry Emery 2/23/93	Sean Fermoyle 4/4/2000
Gerard Babakian 1/19/2001	Ed Benguiat 1/1/64 l	Thad Boss 1/19/2001	Lynn Cabot-Puro 9/21/99	Len Cheeseman 10/25/93	Kyle Cooper 8/14/97	Susan Darbyshire 1/1/87	Jonathan Doney 2/7/96	Stefan Engelhardt 1/19/2001	Antero Ferreira 8/14/97
Roberto Bagatti 6/18/2001	Lars Bergquist 1/19/2001	Jaime Boyle 7/20/99 s	Joanne Cadovius 10/25/99 s	David Cheung,Jr. 5/7/98	Rodrigo Corral 7/21/98	Karen Davidson 1/19/2001	Lou Dorfsman 1/1/54 l	Fabienne Erni 3/1/2001 s	Louise Fili 4/4/2000

HELLO my name is	HELLO my name is	HELLO my name is	HELLO my name is	HELLO my name is	HELLO my name is	HELLO my name is	HELLO my name is	HELLO my name is	HELLO my name is
Simon Fitton 1/27/94	G	Austin Grandjean 1/1/59	William Hafeman 6/24/96	Kathy Hettinga 1/19/2001	Eva Hueckmann 4/2/2001	K	Claus Koch 11/5/96	L	Herbert Lenzner 9/21/99
James Fitzgerald 11/6/2000	Christof Gassner 9/1/90	Stefanie Grashoff 6/30/99	Allan Haley 1/1/78	Michael Heu 1/31/2000	Gerard Huerta 1/1/85	Otso Kallinen 4/4/2000	Jesse Taylor Koechling 1/29/98	Gerry L'Orange 4/30/91	Olaf Leu 1/1/66
Kristine Fitzgerald 11/27/90	Martina Gates 12/10/96	Stephen Green 8/14/97	Crystal Hall 2/4/97	Eric Heubel 12/28/2000	David Hukari 11/7/95	John Kallio 2/7/96	Daniel Kolchinsky	Raymond F. Laccetti 1/1/87	Patrick Leung 8/23/2000
Robert Fleck 3/1/2001	David Gatti 1/1/81	Karen Greenberg 6/21/95	Debra Hall 9/20/96	Fons M. Hickmann 9/20/96	Harvey Hunt 10/1/92	Mie Kashiwagi 3/1/2001	Jessica Koman 1/19/2001	Regina Lamberti 3/1/2001	Randi Davis Levin 12/11/2000
Gonçalo Fonseca 1/1/93	Matthew Gaynor 12/6/99	Ariel Grey 4/4/2000	Angelica Hamann 3/1/2001	Jay Higgins 1/1/88		Nan Keeton 1/1/97	Steve Kopec 1/1/74	Melchior Lamy 3/1/2001	Adam Levite 11/6/97
Wayne Ford 3/6/96	Kai Gehrmann 11/5/96	James Grieshaber 9/20/96	Egil Haraldsen 5/8/2000	Elise Hilpert 11/6/2000	I	Brunette Kenan 9/21/99	Matthias Kott 11/5/96	John Langdon 8/12/93	Renee Levitt 4/2/98
Margaret Kane Forgosh 9/21/99	Frank Germano 1/19/2001	Frank E. E. Grubich 6/24/96	Keith Harris 11/12/98	Helmut Himmler 11/5/96	Yanek Iontef 2/28/2000	Kay Khoo 1/7/99	Marcus Kraus 8/14/97	Guenter Gerhard Lange 1/1/83	Richard S. Levy 9/21/99
Dan Forster 7/17/2000	Robyn Gill-Attaway 10/25/93	Rosanne Guararra 4/1/92	Knut Hartmann 1/1/85	Norihiko Hirata 11/5/96	Elizabeth Irwin 10/4/2000	Jang Hoon Kim 11/6/97	Stephanie Kreber 3/1/2001	Terje Langeggen 5/7/98	Katherine Leyton 5/8/2000
Thomas Fowler 9/13/93	Lou Glassheim 1/1/47	Ivan Guarini 4/2/2001	Judi Haviland 10/4/2000	J. Drew Hodges 6/21/95	Terry Irwin 6/24/96	June Hyung Kim 11/6/2000	Bernhard J. Kress 1/1/63	Jean Larcher 1/19/2001	Jan Lindquist 6/18/2001
Alessandro Franchini 6/24/96	Howard Glener 1/1/77	Grace Guarte 5/8/2000	Helen Hayes 5/7/98	Michael Hodgson 1/1/89		Yeunkyum Kim 10/4/2000	Peter Kruty 10/25/99	Marcia Lausen 3/1/2001	Kuan Ling 10/4/2000
Henrik-Jan Francke 1/19/2001	Carin Goldberg 8/14/97	Christiane Gude 11/6/97	Bonnie Hazelton 1/1/75	Jonathan Hoefler 5/8/2000	J	Richard King 1/31/2000	Walter Kryshak 12/11/2000	David Lawter 4/2/2001	Miles Markum Linklater 5/7/98
Artur Frankowski 12/11/2000	Giuliano Cesar Gonçalves 1/19/2001	Olga Gutierrez de la Roza 9/12/95	Amy Hecht 3/1/2001	Fritz Hofrichter 1/1/80	Donald Jackson 1/1/78	Rick King 6/26/93	Toshiyuki Kudo 7/17/2000	James Lebbad 6/18/2001	Christine Linnehan 3/1/2001
Carol Freed 1/1/87	Ronnen Goren 8/14/97	Einar Gylfason 9/12/95	Frank Heine 2/7/96	Troy Holder 10/25/99	Ed Jacobus 3/1/2001	Paul Kingett 11/6/2000	Felix Kunkler 6/18/2001	David W. Lecours 12/6/99	Monica Little 4/2/98
Hugh Werner Freitas 8/23/2000	Holly Goscinsky 4/2/98	Peter Gyllan 11/6/97	Arne Heine 12/11/2000	Roman Holt 6/30/99	Michael Jager 9/20/94	Alexander Knowlton 6/24/96	Christian Kunnert 6/10/97	Cindy Lee 8/23/2000	Wally Littman 1/1/60
Tobias Frere-Jones 5/8/2000	Edward Gottschall 11/1/52		Wild Heinz 9/20/96	Shannon Holt 1/19/2001	Mark Jamra 10/25/99	Cynthia Knox 6/21/95	Ralf Kunz 2/23/93	Jae Lee 5/3/2001	Esther Liu 4/2/98
Adrian Frutiger 1/1/67	Norman Graber 1/1/69	H	Earl M. Herrick 6/24/96	Kevin Horvath 1/1/87	David R. Jennings 4/2/2001	Akira Kobayashi 7/20/99	Kuang Chun Kuo 5/6/97	Susan Jeehoon Lee 8/14/97	Lorena Llaneza 4/2/98
Mario Fuhr 8/14/97	Diana Graham 12/1/84	Tomi Haaparanta 1/19/2001	Klaus Hesse 3/7/95	Anton Huber 1/19/2001	Andy Johnson 3/8/99	Nana Kobayashi 3/6/96	Yoshiko Kusaka 11/6/97	David Lemon 6/21/95	Doug Lockyer 10/25/99
HELLO my name is	HELLO my name is	HELLO my name is	HELLO my name is	HELLO my name is	HELLO my name is	HELLO my name is	HELLO my name is	HELLO my name is	HELLO my name is

HELLO my name is

Uwe Loesch 9/20/96	Julie Markfield 1/19/2001	Uwe Melichar 1/31/2000	Richard Earl Moore 1/1/82	Raymond Nichols 1/19/2001	Michel Olivier 1/27/94	Daniel Pelavin 9/1/92	R	Erik Ries 12/6/99	Timothy J. Ryan 6/24/96
Beng Hew Loh 3/1/2001	Rosemary Markowsky 11/12/98	Dr. Frieder Mellinghoff 12/6/99	Minoru Morita 1/1/75	Maria Nicklin 1/19/2001	Erik Olsen 1/19/2001	Robert Peters 1/1/86	Jochen Raedeker 12/11/2000	Robert Rindler 9/12/95	Carol-Anne Ryce-Paul 4/2/2001
John Howland Lord 1/1/47	Lindsey Marshall 4/2/2001	Jeff Merrells 10/4/2000	John Michael Morris 9/10/98	Charles Nix 11/6/2000	Hui Ming Ong 5/8/2000	Oanh Pham-Phu 6/24/96	Erwin Raith 1/1/67	Phillip Ritzenberg 11/6/97	Michael Rylander 6/26/93
Alexander Luckow 1/27/94	Igor Masnjak 1/29/98	Frederic Metz 1/1/85	Lars Müller 2/4/97	Shuichi Nogami 8/14/97	Robert Overholtzer 3/10/94	Ken Phillips 9/21/99	Renee Ramsey-Passmore 6/30/99	Jose Rivera 1/19/2001	
Frank Luedicke 9/21/99	Michelle Mason 8/14/97	David Michaelides 11/6/97	Joachim Muller-Lancé 9/12/95	Brian Nolan 11/6/2000		Max Phillips 5/8/2000	Sal Randazzo 7/17/2000	Rich Roat 6/30/99	S
Gregg Lukasiewicz 11/18/90	Joanne Matthews 10/4/2000	Tony Mikolajczyk 2/4/97	Gary Munch 11/6/97	Gertrud Nolte 1/19/2001	P	Clive Piercy 6/24/96	Matthew Rascoff 1/19/2001	Nadine Robbins 11/7/95	Greg Sadowski 3/1/2001
Linnea Lundquist 12/6/99	Andreas Maxbauer 9/12/95	John Milligan 1/1/78	Jerry King Musser 1/1/88	Alexa Nosal 1/1/87	Norman Paege 11/28/99	Ian Pilbeam 12/6/99	Nikki Rasheed 5/3/2001	Angel Roberts 11/6/2000	Gus Saelens 1/1/50
Matt Lynch 3/1/2001	Eileen McCarren 5/8/2000	Michael Miranda 1/1/84	Alexander Musson 9/13/93		Frank Paganucci 1/1/85	Margaret Piscitelli 5/8/2000	Marcus Ratliff 9/21/99	Chad Roberts 1/19/2001	Ilja Sallacz 9/21/99
	Rod McDonald 11/7/95	Oswaldo Miranda (Miran) 1/1/78	Louis A. Musto 1/1/65	O	Aubree Pappas 7/21/98	Albert-Jan Pool 10/4/2000	Bob Rauchman 8/14/97	Eva Roberts 9/12/95	David Saltman 1/1/66
M	Jon McGrew 1/19/2001	Ralf Mischnick 5/7/98		Mary Ellen O'Boyle 11/6/2000	Enrique Pardo 5/10/99	Lisa Powers 6/24/96	Jo Anne Redwood 1/1/88	Frank Rocholl 3/8/99	Ina Saltz 6/24/96
Burns Magruder 1/31/2000	Barbara McKenzie 1/19/2001	Dean Mitchell 2/28/2000	N	Nicole B. O'Connor 9/21/99	Sharon Mee Sun Park 6/18/2001	Will Powers 1/1/89	Hans Dieter Reichert 5/1/92	Salvador Romero 11/30/93	Rodrigo Sanchez 6/24/96
Danusch Mahmoudi 4/2/2001	Marc A. Meadows 6/24/96	Susan Mitchell 7/21/98	Cristiana Neri-Downey 8/14/97	Oisin O'Malley 1/29/98	Jim Parkinson 9/20/94	Randal Presson 1/19/2001	Crystal Reid 1/19/2001	Edward Rondthaler 1/1/47	Alejandra Santos 6/21/2000
Heidi Makino 6/18/2001	Donna Meadows Manier 6/30/99	Michael Moesslang 12/6/99	Helmut Ness 12/6/99	Jack Odette 1/1/77	Guy Pask 8/14/97	Richard Price 1/31/2000	Liz Reitman 6/10/97	Kurt Roscoe 1/1/93	Stephanie Sassola-Struse 2/4/97
Ohsugi Manabu 1/19/2001	Gabriel Martinez Meave	Sakol Mongkolka-setarin 6/21/95	Robert Newman 6/24/96	Ninja V. Oertzen 1/7/99	Kim Paulsen 1/19/2001	Vittorio Prina 1/1/88	Heather L. Reitze 1/19/2001	Gabriela Rotaru 4/4/2000	Nathan Savage 1/19/2001
Marilyn Marcus 1/1/79	Roland Mehler 1/1/85	James Montalbano 10/25/93	David Ng 10/4/2000	Akio Okumura 11/5/96	Gudrun Pawelke 6/24/96	James Propp 6/10/97	Peter Retallick 8/23/2000	Gil Rukenstein 5/8/2000	John Sayles 9/12/95
Ari Mardewi 11/6/97	Friederike Meissner 4/4/2000	Joseph Montebello 6/24/96	Lillian Ng 5/8/2000	Scott Olason 12/6/99	B. Martin Pedersen 1/1/85	Richard Puder 1/1/85	James T. Rhoades 4/12/99	Paul Rustand 6/30/99	David Saylor 6/24/96
Marie Mariucci 1/29/98		Christine Moog 9/21/99	Bonnie Nicolas 5/3/2001	Hope Olenyik 8/23/2000	Adam Robert Peele 1/19/2001		Fabian Richter 1/19/2001	Erkki Ruuhinen 1/1/86	Hartmut Schaarschmidt 1/19/2001

HELLO my name is **Matthias Schäfer** 8/14/97 s
HELLO my name is **Joerg Sebald** 4/2/2001 s
HELLO my name is **Bill Smith** 1/19/2001
HELLO my name is **William Streever** 1/1/50 l
HELLO my name is **Jack Tauss** 1/1/75
HELLO my name is **Vivanne Tubiana** 4/2/2001
HELLO my name is **Michelle Van Santen** 1/19/2001
HELLO my name is **Xu Wang** 8/12/93
HELLO my name is **James Williams** 1/1/88
HELLO my name is **Ronald Yeung** 1/31/2000

HELLO my name is **Hans Dirk Schellnack** 6/18/2001
HELLO my name is **James Sebastian** 6/21/95
HELLO my name is **James C. Smith** 5/7/97
HELLO my name is **Ilene Strizver** 1/1/88
HELLO my name is **Pat Taylor** 1/1/85
HELLO my name is **Marc Tulke** 8/23/2000
HELLO my name is **Janine Vangoo** 11/19/2001
HELLO my name is **Jane Ward** 5/7/98
HELLO my name is **Joseph R. Williams** 7/21/98 s
HELLO my name is **Cheng Yu-Pin** 3/1/2001

HELLO my name is **Martin Schitto** 4/2/2001
HELLO my name is **Enrico Sempi** 8/14/97
HELLO my name is **Silvestre Segarra Soler** 11/7/95
HELLO my name is **Matthew J. Strong** 7/21/98
HELLO my name is **Lisa Marie Taylor** 8/14/97
HELLO my name is **James Tung** 5/30/97
HELLO my name is **Yury Vargas** 1/7/99
HELLO my name is **Janet Webb** 6/1/91
HELLO my name is **Tom Williams** 5/8/2000
HELLO my name is **Z**

HELLO my name is **Peter Schlief** 12/11/2000 s
HELLO my name is **Scott Severson** 8/23/2000
HELLO my name is **Martin Solomon** 1/1/55 l
HELLO my name is **Vance Studley** 9/12/95
HELLO my name is **Anthony J. Teano** 1/1/62
HELLO my name is **Ryan Tungseth** 8/23/2000
HELLO my name is **Anna Villano** 4/12/99 s
HELLO my name is **Harald Weber** 6/30/99
HELLO my name is **Caroline Winata** 1/31/2000
HELLO my name is **Hermann Zapf** 1/1/52 h

HELLO my name is **Hermann Schlieper** 1/1/87
HELLO my name is **Jessica Shatan** 11/7/95
HELLO my name is **Jan Solpera** 1/1/85
HELLO my name is **Katja Stuke** 2/4/97
HELLO my name is **Ana Teixeira** 9/10/98
HELLO my name is **Francois Turcotte** 1/7/99
HELLO my name is **Annette von Brandis** 9/20/96 s
HELLO my name is **Matt Weber** 3/5/98
HELLO my name is **Grant Windridge** 8/23/2000
HELLO my name is **David Zauhar** 6/18/2001

HELLO my name is **Holger Schmidhuber** 12/6/99
HELLO my name is **Paul Shaw** 1/1/87
HELLO my name is **Ronnie Tan Chye Soo** 1/1/88
HELLO my name is **Hansjorg Stulle** 1/1/87
HELLO my name is **Regine Thienhaus** 2/7/96
HELLO my name is **Michael Tutino** 4/24/96
HELLO my name is **Thilo von Debschitz** 11/7/95
HELLO my name is **Joy Weeeng** 1/1/93 s
HELLO my name is **Carol Winer** 7/11/94
HELLO my name is **Stephen Zhang** 1/19/2001

HELLO my name is **Hermann Schmidt** 1/1/83
HELLO my name is **Mark E. Shaw** 9/21/99
HELLO my name is **Brian Sooy** 9/10/98
HELLO my name is **Melissa Sunjaya** 6/30/99
HELLO my name is **Wayne Tidswell** 9/20/96
HELLO my name is **U**
HELLO my name is **Axel Voss** 1/29/98
HELLO my name is **Prof. Kurt Weidemann** 1/1/66 l
HELLO my name is **Conny J. Winter** 1/1/85
HELLO my name is **Maxim Zhukov** 4/24/96

HELLO my name is **Klaus Schmidt** 1/1/59 l
HELLO my name is **Jieun Shin** 7/20/99
HELLO my name is **Erik Spiekermann** 1/1/88
HELLO my name is **Derek Sussner** 6/21/95
HELLO my name is **Fred Tieken** 6/21/95
HELLO my name is **Caroline Ulrich** 3/1/2001
HELLO my name is **W**
HELLO my name is **Claus F. Weidmueller** 3/4/97
HELLO my name is **Penina Wissner** 9/20/96
HELLO my name is **Roy Zucca** 1/1/69

HELLO my name is **Markus Schmidt** 4/20/93
HELLO my name is **Kim Shkapich** 11/6/97
HELLO my name is **Julie Spivey** 10/4/2000
HELLO my name is **Zempaku Suzuki** 7/28/92
HELLO my name is **Eric Tilley** 5/16/95
HELLO my name is **Scott Wadler** 9/12/95
HELLO my name is **Sylvia Weimer** 1/19/2001
HELLO my name is **Delve Withrington** 11/6/97
HELLO my name is **Jeff Zwerner** 8/14/97

HELLO my name is **Bertram Schmidt-Friderichs** 1/1/89
HELLO my name is **Philip Shore** 7/28/92
HELLO my name is **Frank Stahlberg** 10/4/2000
HELLO my name is **Laurie Szujewska** 11/7/95
HELLO my name is **Colin Tillyer** 8/14/97
HELLO my name is **V**
HELLO my name is **Frank Wagner** 7/11/94
HELLO my name is **Patrick Weir** 6/30/99
HELLO my name is **Peter C. Wong** 6/24/96

HELLO my name is **Helmut Schmitt-Siegel** 8/14/97
HELLO my name is **Eric Shropshire** 1/19/2001
HELLO my name is **Rolf Staudt** 1/1/84
HELLO my name is **Alicia Szwec** 6/30/99 s
HELLO my name is **Anton Tilo** 1/29/98
HELLO my name is **Diego Vainesman** 9/1/91
HELLO my name is **Oliver Wagner** 1/19/2001
HELLO my name is **Elizabeth Welsh** 4/2/2001
HELLO my name is **Anuthin Wongsunkakon** 4/2/98
sustaining members

HELLO my name is **Werner Schneider** 1/1/87
HELLO my name is **Mark Simkins** 1/1/92
HELLO my name is **Thomas Stecko** 12/21/94
HELLO my name is **T**
HELLO my name is **Eugene Timerman** 9/21/99
HELLO my name is **Patrick Vallé** 6/30/99
HELLO my name is **Allan R. Wahler** 1/29/98
HELLO my name is **Justin Wendel** 1/19/2001 s
HELLO my name is **Peter Wood** 4/8/97
HELLO my name is **Agfa Monotype** 6/24/96

HELLO my name is **Geraldine Schoeller** 2/7/96
HELLO my name is **Scott Simmons** 7/11/94
HELLO my name is **Lee Steele** 12/11/2000
HELLO my name is **Kan Tai-Keung** 8/14/97
HELLO my name is **Martin Ko Tin-Yau** 1/19/2001
HELLO my name is **Christine Van Bree** 4/2/98
HELLO my name is **Jurek Wajdowicz** 1/1/80
HELLO my name is **Judy Wert** 12/10/96
HELLO my name is **Jon Woodhams** 1/31/2000
HELLO my name is **Galapagos Design Group, Inc.** 6/24/96

HELLO my name is **Eileen Hedy Schultz** 1/1/85
HELLO my name is **Mae Skidmore** 7/21/98
HELLO my name is **Olaf Stein** 4/24/96
HELLO my name is **Douglas Tait** 4/2/98
HELLO my name is **Laura Tolkow** 6/24/96
HELLO my name is **Mark Van Bronkhorst** 9/13/93
HELLO my name is **Sergio Waksman** 6/24/96
HELLO my name is **Paul Wharton** 6/24/96
HELLO my name is **Fred Woodward** 6/21/95
s: student member

HELLO my name is **Lauren Schulz** 7/21/98 s
HELLO my name is **Finn Skødt** 5/8/2000
HELLO my name is **Charles Stewart** 7/28/92
HELLO my name is **Yukichi Takada** 9/12/95
HELLO my name is **Klaus Trommer** 9/21/99
HELLO my name is **Kevin Vander Leek** 8/14/97
HELLO my name is **Susan Waksmonski** 6/24/96
HELLO my name is **Alex White** 4/20/93
HELLO my name is **Laura Coe Wright** 1/7/99
l: life members

HELLO my name is **Eckehart Schumacher-Gebler** 1/1/85
HELLO my name is **Martha Rice Skogen** 6/30/99
HELLO my name is **Charles Stone** 1/19/2001
HELLO my name is **Yoshimaru Takahashi** 9/20/96
HELLO my name is **Niklaus Troxler** 8/23/2000
HELLO my name is **Jan Van Der Ploeg** 1/1/52 l
HELLO my name is **Garth Walker** 7/28/92
HELLO my name is **Albert L. Whitley, Jr.** 4/2/98 s
HELLO my name is **Y**
h: honorary member

HELLO my name is **Jo Scraba** 5/6/97
HELLO my name is **Pat Sloan** 1/1/97
HELLO my name is **Sumner Stone** 1/1/88
HELLO my name is **Keith Tam** 7/17/2000 s
HELLO my name is **Minao Tsukada** 2/4/2000
HELLO my name is **Ryan Van Meter** 9/21/99
HELLO my name is **Stephan Walter** 3/1/2001
HELLO my name is **Richard Wilde** 4/20/93
HELLO my name is **Chien-Hui Yang** 11/6/2000
As of June 2001

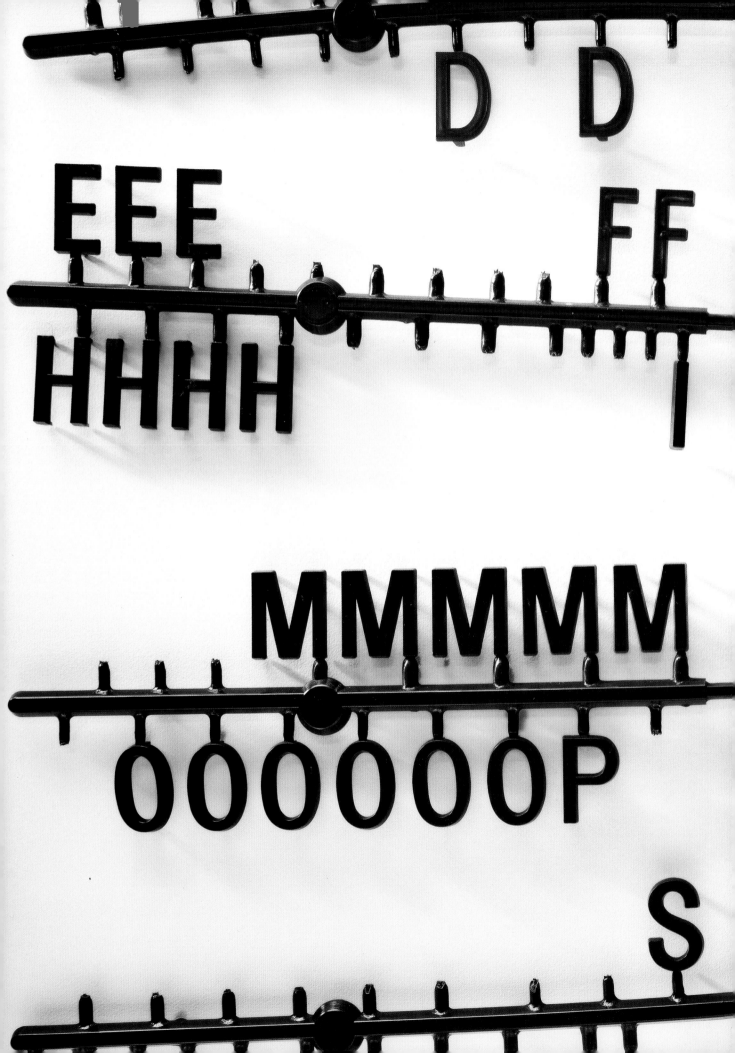

TYPOGRAPHIC INDEX

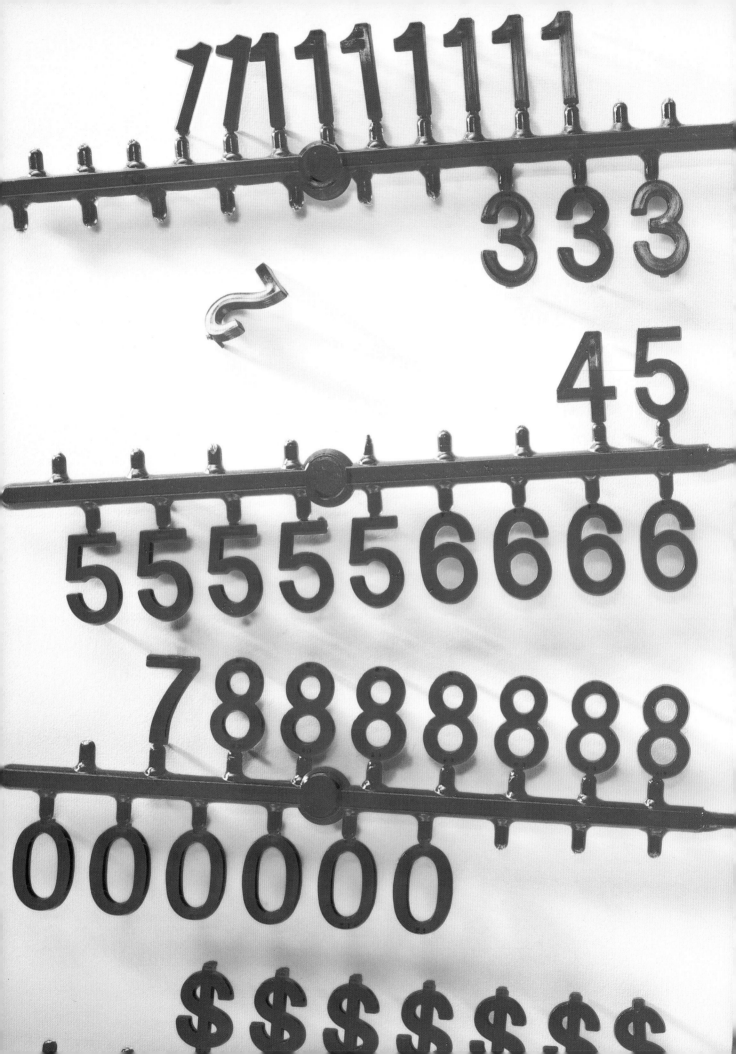

GENERAL INDEX

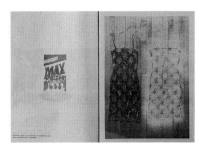

CORRECTION
TYPOGRAPHY 21

DESIGN	Stefan Sagmeister, Martin Woodtli, and Hjati Karlsson *New York, New York*
CREATIVE DIRECTION	Stefan Sagmeister
LETTERING	Stefan Sagmeister and Martin Woodtli
PHOTOGRAPHY	Tom Schierlitz
DESIGN OFFICE	Sagmeister Inc.
CLIENT	Anni Kuan Design
PRINCIPAL TYPE	Handlettering
DIMENSIONS	15 3/4 x 20 in. (40 x 50.8 cm)